ALSO BY LORI LONGBOTHAM

Luscious Lemon Desserts

Lemon Zest

THE

Scoop

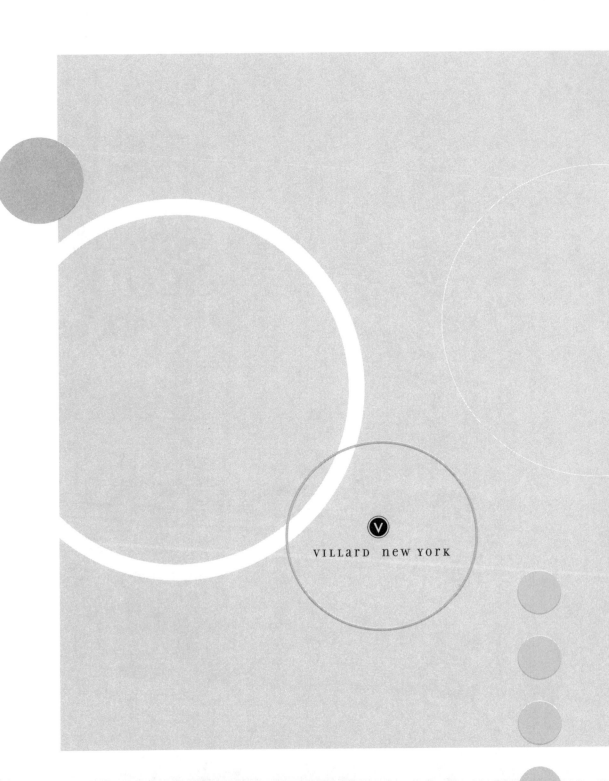

villard new york

THE

Scoop

HOW TO CHANGE STORE-BOUGHT ICE CREAM

INTO FABULOUS DESSERTS

Lori Longbotham

LIBRARY OF CONGRESS CATALOGING-IN-PUBLICATION DATA
Longbotham, Lori.
The scoop: how to change store-bought ice cream into
fabulous desserts / Lori Longbotham.
p. cm.
ISBN 0-375-76082-2
1. Ice cream, ices, etc.   2. Frozen desserts.   I. Title.
TX795 .L76 2003
641.8'62—dc21   2002029634

Villard Books website address: www.villard.com
Printed in the United States of America on acid-free paper
9 8 7 6 5 4 3 2
FIRST EDITION

Book design by Barbara M. Bachman

For Mom, Steve, and Auntie Jean

My advice to you is not to inquire why
or whither but just enjoy your ice cream while
it's on your plate—that's my philosophy.

✳

—THORNTON WILDER, *THE SKIN OF OUR TEETH*, ACT 1

acknowledgments

Enormous thanks to Angela Miller, Mary Bahr, and Judith Sutton—all are lovely and fun, and were vital to *The Scoop* and to me while I was working on it. Thanks also to Beth Pearson, the elegant Misa Erder, Barbara M. Bachman, Laura Johansen, Liz Duffy and Judi Orlick, and Cathy Cook, who found such great scoops.

I would also like to offer thanks and appreciation to Jerry Goldman, Deborah Mintcheff, Barbara Ottenhoff, Barbara Howe, Marie Regusis, Sarah Mahoney, Jean Galton, Sabra Turnbull, Valerie Cipollone, Carol Kramer, Lisa Troland, Tracey Seaman, Susan Westmoreland, Debby Goldsmith, Cathy Lo, Rosanne Toroian, Pat Dailey, David Bailey, Susie Quick, Jena Myers and her parents, Scott Smiley, Jennifer Wehrle, Helen Dell, the Goldmans, Emma Lewis, and, as always, Rosie and Sprocket.

contents

few things in life are as universally adored as ice cream—ice cream and its cousins are everyone's favorite temptation. Nearly everyone smiles at the mere mention of ice cream, and it's amazingly versatile, suited to all occasions, no matter how formal or casual. Americans long ago adopted it as one of our national foods, and lately we have opened our hearts to European-style sorbets and gelatos as well.

Having spent much of my life dedicated to researching the subject, I am convinced that, nowadays, store-bought ice cream is almost always better than homemade. Ice creams, gelatos, frozen yogurts, sorbets, etc., are among the best store-bought products we have. Before the availability of premium brands, store-bought ice cream was always pumped full of air, ingredients were often artificial, and the choice of flavors was extremely limited. It made sense then to churn your own, but now that extremely high-quality ice cream can be found at stores everywhere, what's the point? (And who has time?) The abundance of readily available delicious ice creams, sorbets, and other frozen desserts—and the sauces and toppings to go with them— gives any busy cook a huge head start on dessert.

There are times when you just want to eat your ice cream right out of the container standing in front of the freezer, but the simple guidelines provided here will help you on the occasions when you want something more. This book will allow you to concentrate on the *fun* part of dessert making. Store-bought ice cream, sorbet, gelato, and frozen yogurt can form the basis of a wide variety of assembled desserts—luscious cakes, sundaes, soda fountain drinks, pies and tarts, terrines, and bombes, among others. You can also look forward to mixing and matching those ice creams and so on with homemade or store-bought sauces, toppings, syrups, and garnishes of all sorts.

None of the recipes here are labor-intensive—in fact, even teenagers can prepare them. You, the busier-than-ever home cook, will be able to thrill your guests and family with what they really want—and be thrilled by how little time and effort are involved. With the recipes in this book, you can keep it simple, scrumptious, and fun.

For example, try one of the special oval ice cream scoops available to make the simplest dessert look like a restaurant presentation. Imagine elegant "quenelles" of vanilla ice cream (store-bought) arranged on a dinner plate, drizzled with raspberry sauce (from the refrigerator), and sprinkled with toasted hazelnuts (from the freezer). I've included a huge array of other serving suggestions and inspirations, such as using squeeze bottles and paintbrushes like an uptown pastry chef, serving delicate filled ice cream cones upside down in elegant bowls, and molding large and single-serving frozen desserts. I've also provided directions for preparing and using simply beautiful garnishes from chocolate curls and chocolate leaves to crushed candies, nuts, and cookies to crystallized or fresh fruits and flowers. I've included instructions for easy decorating effects, like creating teardrops or squiggles with sauces. And I've suggested specific "serve-withs," such as cookies, candies, and chocolate-dipped fruits.

I've included a guide to pantry ingredients that will ensure that you always have dessert "makin's" on hand, a fun kids' corner, and tips for using the microwave as a tool for making frozen desserts.

In 2000, the per capita ice cream consumption in this country was five gallons a year! Vanilla is still the most popular ice cream flavor, accounting for one of every four gallons sold. Chocolate is a distant second, followed by nutty flavors in ice cream and fruit flavors in yogurt.

A few tips:

- Because we all love vanilla so much, I based many of these desserts on vanilla ice cream, but you can use any flavor you like—I list many other possibilities too.

- Because we are lucky enough to have European-style sorbets and *sorbettos* available everywhere, I don't use a lot of sherbets. Sherbets are often made with artificial flavorings and colorings, and I think their texture is inferior to sorbets'. But if you love sherbets, use them anytime instead of the sorbets.
- Also, anytime ice cream is in the ingredient list, you can use reduced-fat, nonfat, calcium-fortified, and/or sugar-free ice cream, frozen yogurt, or gelato.

Even the most elaborate of these scrumptious ice cream specialties are far easier to prepare than their grand appearance might suggest. And you don't have to worry about mistakes with these recipes. How bad could a tablespoon "too much" of hot fudge sauce be? (And who decides what's too much?) Think of these recipes as basic guidelines, or formulas, and, above all, have fun!

*t*here are many maybes and much conflicting information about the history of ice cream, with a good deal of myth and folklore surrounding the subject. The most likely theory is that ice cream evolved from iced drinks, maybe from iced wine. As long ago as four centuries before Christ, documents describe Alexander the Great as fond of iced beverages. And there are records indicating that in A.D. 62, the Roman emperor Nero sent fleets of ships to the mountains of the Apennines to "harvest" ice and snow, which he enjoyed flavored with fruit juices, fruit pulp, and honey.

Iced dairy products are mentioned in ancient Chinese literature dating to the twelfth century, and water ices are thought to have been enjoyed throughout Asia for thousands of years. Marco Polo is said to have brought recipes for water ices to Europe from the East, and when Catherine de' Medici married Henry II and became queen of France in 1533, she brought her chefs and, along with them, their recipes for *sorbetto*.

In the mid-1600s, the combination of ice and salt (to depress the freezing point) was used as a way of producing frozen desserts, namely ices. By 1660, the first café in Paris, Café Procope, was selling water ices, and some say cream ices were also made and sold there.

Frozen desserts then made their way to America, and in 1700, Governor Bladen of Maryland was serving ice cream to his guests. The first ice cream parlor opened in New York City in 1776, but until the mid-1800s, ice cream was a rare and exotic treat enjoyed mostly by the very wealthy. Dolley Madison had strawberry ice cream served as one of the desserts at the second inaugural ball in 1812.

The first hand-cranked freezer was invented by Philadelphia housewife Nancy Johnson and patented in 1843. Between 1848 and 1873, sixty-nine other patents were issued for hand-cranked ice cream freezers. The first commercial ice cream plant was established in Baltimore by Jacob Fussell in 1851; until then, most ice cream was made at home or at concession stands, where it was enjoyed on the spot.

The ice cream cone is attributed (by some, at least) to Italo Marchiony, who immigrated from Italy in the late 1800s, and is said to have produced the first ice cream cone, in 1896 in New York City. In December 1903, he was granted a patent for his special mold.

*f*irst the ingredients for the ice cream mix are blended in a mixing tank.
Besides milk, cream, sugar, eggs, and flavoring, the mix may contain small amounts of
ingredients such as a stabilizer, which prevents the formation of ice crystals in the ice cream.

The mix then goes to a pasteurizer, where it is heated and held at a precise
temperature for a specific period of time. The most common type of pasteurization is the high-temperature–short-time method, in which the mix is heated to 175 degrees F and held there for
25 seconds. The hot mix then goes to the homogenizer, where, under pressure of 2,000 to 2,500
pounds per square inch, the milk fat globules are broken into smaller particles, which will help
make the ice cream smooth.

After homogenization, the mix is quickly cooled to a temperature of about 40
degrees F. Freezing the mix is accomplished by using one of two devices: a continuous freezer,
which freezes mix that moves through it in a steady flow, or a batch freezer, which makes a
single quantity of ice cream at a time. As the ice cream is being frozen, blades in the freezer,
or dashers, whip and aerate the mix. Without this aeration, the ice cream would be an inedible
solidly frozen mass of cream, milk, sugar, and flavoring. In this country, the amount of aeration,
called overrun, is controlled by federal regulations; ice cream must not weigh less than four and
a half pounds per gallon.

With a continuous freezer, ingredients such as fruits, nuts, and cookie dough
are added after freezing by a mechanical flavor feeder. Liquid flavors are added to the mix prior
to freezing.

After being packed in cartons, the ice cream goes to the "hardening room," where subzero temperatures further harden the ice cream. From there, it is loaded onto refrigerated trucks to begin its journey to our tables.

*Y*ou don't need to make any enormous or overwhelming evaluations or investments, like choosing between a hand-crank or electric ice cream machine; your biggest decision will be which ice cream scoop, or scoops, to buy.

Scoops for ice cream are divided into two categories: spades and dippers. Spades are wide, flat, shovel-shaped utensils, usually in one piece. They are good for scooping flat slabs of ice cream for filling pies or molds, or for forming a garnish that won't roll off a slice of pie or cake. Spades are also just what you need to swirl different flavors of frozen desserts together. Arrange thin layers removed with the spade around a layer of another flavor. Try it with vanilla ice cream and raspberry sorbet, and then branch out.

There are basically two different styles of dippers, sometimes known as dishers. One is a half-moon-shaped stainless-steel dipper with a spring-operated thumb-release ejection mechanism. The other type looks like a very sturdy spoon with a thick handle; this type may be nonstick for quick release or filled with a core of self-defrosting fluid, like antifreeze, for easy scooping. My favorite brand of the latter type is Zeroll, which is widely available.

The classic type, with the quick-release lever, originally came in nine sizes, ranging from number 6 to number 40. (The lower the number, the larger the bowl.) In theory, the numbers referred to how many scoops of ice cream you could dip from a quart, but in reality there are many other factors at play—such as your dipping technique and how much air the ice cream contains. Some of these scoops will be too large for a pint container.

As dippers are available in many shapes, materials, and sizes, you might want to pick up a couple. Keep in mind what size portions you intend to serve and the shapes you like best. Consider an oval scoop for making egg, or quenelle, shapes—they add elegance with no extra work. You can also make oval scoops using two tablespoons: Scoop up an oval of softened ice cream with one spoon, slide the second one over the ice cream, transfer it to the second spoon, and shape it into an oval, then repeat the process and gently ease the oval onto a plate. (Tablespoons can also be used to make shavings of softened ice cream or other frozen desserts if you press them only slightly into the surface and drag them along at a 45-degree angle.)

Melon ballers are useful for making smaller scoops of ice cream, which can look very attractive. They are available with oval and round bowls. To form a ball, press the upturned bowl into slightly softened ice cream, then rotate it to form a perfectly round shape. Then just pile the balls up in a dish or arrange them on a plate. They look particularly lovely arranged with fresh fruits—you could even try arranging the balls on a flat plate in the shape of a bunch of grapes and garnishing them with mint leaves. Or try tiny balls of raspberry or other sorbet on a plate that has been flooded with mango sauce, and tuck in a few fresh raspberries.

Whichever type you use, let the scoop do most of the work. It's always easier to scoop if the ice cream has been softened briefly in the refrigerator. Keep a glass of warm water handy, to use for warming the dipper. Use moderate pressure, and rather than digging down into the ice cream, dip the scoop's "nose" in at a 45-degree angle. Draw the scoop toward you in an arc, skimming the surface until you get a smooth, round ball, and lift out the scoop. To release the ice cream, gently touch it to the dish or cone, and press the release mechanism, if there is one. If topping a cone, finish by gently pressing the back of the dipper against the ice cream to make it stick, taking care not to break the cone or mash the ice cream.

You can "double dip" by half-filling your dipper with one flavor of ice cream and completing the scoop with another. This makes for an attractive marbleized effect.

Scooping in advance can really come in handy. If you're serving many people, or if you're serving warm pastry with cold ice cream, for example, or performing another "temperature-sensitive" task, make your life easier by scooping all the ice cream you will need and arranging the scoops on a chilled wax-paper-lined plate or baking sheet. Cover tightly and freeze until ready to serve. You can roll the scoops in toasted shredded coconut, chopped nuts, crushed candy, or the like before freezing.

spatulas

Both rubber and metal spatulas are indispensable for making ice cream desserts, especially for smoothing layers. You'll find several recipes, many in the ice cream cake and pie chapter, that call for offset spatulas. These are the long, narrow metal type (not the wider pancake-turner type), with blades that are set at an angle. A regular metal spatula can be used if you don't have an offset, but the angle of an offset can be very helpful when you are layering and smoothing ice cream in a mold, springform pan, or pie plate.

"scoop skirts"

Rather than forming a perfectly round globe of ice cream, you might prefer to leave a ruffle framing the bottom of the scoop—called a skirt. Just dip the scoop into the ice cream and form a half-orb; don't use the edge of the scoop to cut off the ice cream around the outside of the ball.

What Is Overrun?

Overrun is one of the major differences between premium ice creams and store-brand or economy ice creams. *Overrun* simply means how much air is beaten into the ice cream during the freezing process. If an ice cream mix, or base, were just put into the freezer it would freeze into a hard block that would be both unpleasant to eat and difficult to serve. So, during freezing, the mix is aerated by "dashers," or revolving blades. The air that is incorporated by this whipping action prevents ice cream from becoming a solid mass. The amount of aeration, or overrun, ice cream may contain is regulated by a federal standard that requires that ice cream weigh no less than four and a half pounds per gallon, ensuring that you won't bring home a container of ice cream that is mostly air. However, supermarket-brand ice creams have a much higher overrun than premium ice creams, which are always heavier, denser, and richer. Overrun is a big part of the reason you can buy a half-gallon of store-brand ice cream for about the same amount as a pint of super-premium.

To Buy Premium Ice Cream or Not?

That said, I often use "regular" ice creams. When most of our classic soda fountain treats were devised, there was no such thing as very high-butterfat, low-overrun ice cream, and sometimes a less dense type works better in these desserts. Although many ice cream lovers buy premium ice cream no matter what they are using it for, I recommend considering less-rich ice creams occasionally. Most of these soda fountain classics are fancy and rich enough on their own—they don't need high-butterfat, low-overrun ice cream. I am particularly fond of Breyers ice cream, and it is a very good value; the French vanilla uses no additives and has a superb texture—it slices well in a cake or pie.

It can be beneficial, though certainly not necessary, to use premium ice cream in cakes, ice cream sandwiches, and pies, or in any dessert where the ice cream is softened and then refrozen. The higher butterfat content of premium ice cream can help keep the refrozen ice cream from getting icy.

● *Ice Cream Defined*

According to the "federal standards of identity" for ice cream, it is a frozen food made from a mixture of dairy products, containing a minimum of 10 percent milk fat. It usually has around 130 calories and 7 grams of fat per half-cup.

SUPER-PREMIUM ICE CREAM Although the term is not regulated by the government, super-premium ice cream tends to have a very low overrun and a high fat content; it is usually made with the highest-quality ingredients. Well-known super-premium brands include Häagen-Dazs and Ben & Jerry's. These ice creams range from 150 to 300 calories and 8 to 20 grams of fat per half-cup serving.

PREMIUM ICE CREAM Premium ice cream tends to have a lower overrun and a higher fat content than regular ice cream and to be made with high-quality ingredients.

ECONOMY ICE CREAM Economy ice cream meets the overrun standards, although it has as much air pumped into it as possible under those regulations. It also generally sells for a lower price than regular ice cream.

LIGHT ICE CREAM Also known as "lite" ice cream, this is defined as a frozen food with the fat content reduced by 50 percent, or the calories by 33 percent, in comparison to an average of leading brands or the individual company's own brand of ice cream. These are generally a little higher in fat per serving than products labeled "low-fat." *Light* is always a relative term and one that has no FDA-regulated meaning.

REDUCED-FAT ICE CREAM Also labeled "less-fat" or "lower-fat," reduced-fat ice cream has a fat content reduced by 25 percent in comparison to an average of leading brands or the particular company's own brand of ice cream. Fat content is limited to a maximum of 3 grams per half-cup serving.

FAT-FREE ICE CREAM These ice creams contain virtually no fat, less than 0.5 gram total fat per half-cup serving. Vegetable gums are generally added to make them creamy.

MELLORINE Mellorine is a frozen dessert similar to ice milk, in which the milk fat is replaced, wholly or partially, with vegetable fat. The minimum fat content is 6 percent. It is part of a category called "non-dairy frozen desserts" that includes Tofutti, Rice Dream, Ice Bean, and Mocha Mix. These are good for those who are lactose-intolerant, but note that they can be high or low in fat.

GELATO *Gelato* is the Italian word for ice cream, and it is a soft, rich frozen dessert that has less air than classic American-style ice cream. It is often lower in butterfat too, which seems to allow the flavors to come through more clearly, and to taste purer and fresher. Gelato and ice cream are interchangeable in these recipes.

SORBET Sorbet is a smooth frozen ice usually made with fruit juice or another flavored liquid. Sorbets almost never contain dairy products (except for a sorbet-like crème fraîche).

SHERBET A smooth frozen ice usually made with fruit, sugar, and milk, sherbet typically contains between 1 percent and 2 percent milk fat.

*In the whole array of terms used in the culinary art,
there are few of larger application or more
uncertain meaning than the word* sherbet.

*

—COMPTON DENE (FRED T. VINE),
ICES PLAIN AND FANCY

In the Store

Make the grocery store or ice cream parlor your last errand before going home, and make the ice cream aisle your last stop in the supermarket. If ice cream is kept at a proper temperature, it will be thoroughly frozen and will feel hard to the touch. If it seems soft, you may wish to bring it to the attention of the store manager.

In an open freezer case, always choose ice cream stored below the freezer line.

Insulate the ice cream for the walk or ride home. When your groceries are packed, request a freezer bag or an additional brown paper bag to insulate your ice cream.

At Home

Store ice cream in the main part of the freezer, not in the freezer door, where it will be subject to fluctuating temperatures.

Do not allow ice cream to repeatedly soften and refreeze. If ice cream's small crystals melt and refreeze too often, they will eventually turn into large icy pieces.

Don't store ice cream alongside uncovered foods; it may absorb unwanted odors. If there is ice cream left in the container after serving, top it with wax paper, pressing it right up against the surface of the ice cream, before you cover it with the lid. The wax paper will keep any slightly defrosted ice cream from turning icy.

How to Slightly Soften Ice Cream

It's no fun to wait for ice cream that's too hard to serve. To avoid the problem, transfer it to the refrigerator fifteen to twenty minutes before you'll need it. Thawing it in the refrigerator allows the ice cream to soften more uniformly than it would on the counter, where it's likely to get soft on the outside while remaining hard in the center. Or thaw it briefly in the microwave—a couple of minutes on the defrost setting, or a minute on full power—then leave it at room temperature for five minutes or so.

The higher the overrun—that is, the more air there is in the ice cream—the less time it will take to soften. So premium ice cream will take longer to soften than a store brand.

You don't need to buy special old-fashioned soda, sundae, and "split" dishes for serving ice cream. The dishes and glasses you already have in your cupboard are probably more graceful, up-to-date, and fun than the traditional ones. Whatever bowls, glasses, or plates you use, consider freezing them for a very cool look.

Here are some ideas for you to try:

- Serve frozen desserts in glasses. They look extraordinarily fresh and refreshing.
- Fill iced glasses with sorbets—frosty blue glasses look marvelous with berry sorbets.
- Fill espresso or other coffee cups with ice cream.
- Serve sorbets or ice creams in Champagne coupes, or serve small scoops in Champagne flutes, alternating sorbets and ice creams, or different flavors of either.
- Use colored aluminum glasses or footed bowls.
- Fill several sake cups with different flavors of ice cream and serve together on a square plate. Or try Japanese teacups.
- Use eggcups for serving ice cream or sorbet.
- Serve several flavors of ice cream and/or sorbet in large balloon wineglasses— they make for a much more appealing dessert than heavy sundae dishes.
- Dip the rim of a serving glass in water, then dip into sugar, plain or flavored or colored.
- Serve ice cream in small jelly jars, with cookies on the side.

- Use small ramekins; you could even wrap a foil or parchment collar around the ramekins and fill them above the rim, as you would for a frozen soufflé.
- Serve sorbet, gelato, or ice cream in citrus shells, kiwi shells, tiny pineapple halves, coconut shells, or even pomegranate shells, garnished with pomegranate seeds, of course. Perhaps the grandest way to serve sorbet is the way they do it at Gazelle d'Or in Morocco, where they fill hollowed-out small oranges with orange sorbet flavored with orange-flower water. Before they fill the shells, they cut a small hole in the bottom of each one, thread a pipe cleaner through, and knot it at the base. Then they hang the shells from the branches of small potted trees that are brought to the table, for diners to pick the fruits.

CHOCOLATE-DIPPED TEACUPS OR MUGS

Use either English- or Asian-style teacups, or mugs. If you use cups with handles or mugs, wipe the handles clean after dipping into the chocolate. To serve, scoop ice cream into each dipped cup, and place on a saucer, if using.

MAKES 6 TO 8 DIPPED CUPS

3 ounces bittersweet or semisweet chocolate, finely chopped
¼ cup finely chopped toasted nuts

1. Melt the chocolate in a heatproof bowl set over a saucepan of simmering water, stirring until smooth. Spread the nuts on a plate.
2. Dip the rims of six to eight teacups or mugs in the warm chocolate to give a thick coating, then dip into the nuts until well coated. Let stand, right side up, until the chocolate is set, about 1 hour, depending on the weather.

*b*eyond *the obvious combinations of strawberry ice cream and strawberry* sorbet with tiny ripe fresh strawberries on the stem, and raspberry ice cream with fresh raspberries frosted from a quick trip to the freezer, here are many more garnishes to try.

● *Fruit and Flower Garnishes*

Pit cherries and thread them on wooden skewers. If you freeze them, they will look frosty and inviting. You can do the same with melon balls or small chunks of almost any fruit.

To make strawberry fans, select beautiful dark red berries with the stems attached. Using a sharp paring knife, make several cuts, less than ¼ inch apart, from just below the stem end to the point of each berry, then pinch the base gently to fan out the slices.

Tiny black Corinth grapes, also known as champagne grapes, frozen or not, are a lovely garnish, as are fresh red, black, or white currants on the stem when they're in the market. You can also lightly brush small bunches of these or strawberries, cherries, or other grapes with water, roll or dip into granulated sugar to coat, and allow to dry on a wire rack before using.

For frosted edible flowers, including herb flowers, brush the flowers very lightly with beaten egg white, sprinkle with superfine sugar, and let dry on a wire rack. Use these the same day you make them.

Sprinkle a few glistening fresh pomegranate seeds over a dessert for a dazzling garnish. Or remove a spiral of the red skin from fresh white lychees for a fun and dramatic garnish—or just use drained canned lychees.

Microwave Chocolate-Dipped Strawberries (see page 116) make a graceful garnish. Or try other fruits: dried pear, peach, nectarine, or apricot halves, cherries, figs, orange slices, sliced bananas, or small pineapple wedges.

Be on the lookout for store-bought Granny Smith apple chips. Made by Seneca and available in most supermarkets, these make any dessert look wonderfully professional; simply stand one straight up in a scoop of ice cream. Also look for dried strawberries, gooseberries, and mulberries in specialty food stores; they make lovely garnishes.

Mini or baby pears or baby apples packed in light syrup, available in specialty food stores and some supermarkets, make a terrific garnish. Or try jarred blackberries, sour cherries, black currants, whole white peaches, or gooseberries in syrup, or jarred brandied fruits. Jarred lingonberries in syrup from Scandinavia also make a lovely garnish.

Use diced, sliced, or whole fruit jellies for an eye-catching garnish. Or try guava paste, available in Hispanic markets and some supermarkets, cut into tiny cubes.

Buy good-quality candied citrus peel, or make your own fresh citrus zest garnishes: For corkscrews of zest, remove strips of orange, lemon, and/or lime zest with a channel knife (see sidebar), and wind each strip around a toothpick. Leave it for just a minute or two, then slip off; they will hold their shape on top of or on the side of a dessert.

Or combine minced candied citrus peel and minced crystallized ginger and sprinkle over desserts.

Try store-bought coconut slices, available in specialty food shops and Asian markets. Sliced from a whole coconut, with the thinnest border of the brown skin, they look as if you just cut them from a fresh coconut—and, when they're toasted, they taste like it too.

. . . .

channel knife

A channel knife is a handheld tool with a notched, usually stainless-steel blade that cuts ¼-inch-wide strips of citrus peel. You can remove the peel in one continuous strip, beginning at one end and spiraling around the fruit. The channel knife produces a thick strip of peel, not just the zest, which is great for garnishing. You can twist it decoratively and even tie it into a knot.

. . . .

• *Candy and Chocolate Garnishes*
Crushed or in large pieces, hard caramel, Praline (page xxxix), toffee, or peanut or other nut brittles add a sophisticated look and flavor to ice cream desserts. (You can find toffee bits in bags near the chocolate chips, or use larger pieces, coated in chocolate or not.)

Whole or chopped molasses chips (I grew up loving Mother See's version coated with dark chocolate) have a great texture, perfect for serving with smooth, creamy frozen desserts.

Crush peppermint candies for sprinkling, or garnish individual servings with slender peppermint sticks. Or finely grind hard licorice candy and sprinkle it over desserts for an unusual garnish. Other candy garnishes to consider include diced or whole chocolate-covered mints, tiny peanut butter cups or chopped frozen large cups, chocolate-covered raisins or dried sour cherries, nonpareils, mini chocolate or butterscotch chips, chocolate truffles, and crushed sour lemon or other fruit-flavored hard candies.

You might also try a sprinkle of Ghirardelli sweet ground chocolate, or grind any type of chocolate, even Mexican (available in Latino and specialty food markets), for an easy garnish. Or, for a graceful garnish, look for chocolate lace, available in candy and specialty food shops.

For a simple but grand garnish, mince stem ginger packed in syrup.

Sesame and other nut crunches and crumbled halvah make exotic garnishes. Or try chopped nougat or torrone. The tamarind, nutmeg, mango, or ginger candies available in Asian markets also make an unusual garnish.

For a fun garnish, think of caramel and other flavored popcorns, such as caramel fudge and almond pecan.

● Nut Garnishes

Any nuts, including walnuts (try black walnuts), cashews, almonds, pecans, macadamias, peanuts, pine nuts, pistachios, and even wild hickory nuts, whole, ground, or chopped, can garnish an endless array of ice cream desserts.

Grind pistachios with a pinch of cardamom seeds (not the pods) and a little sugar for an exotic garnish.

For sweet nut garnishes, use pastel-colored Jordan almonds, or be really fancy and use the gold- and/or silver-coated almonds. Or try chocolate-covered almonds, chocolate-cappuccino almonds, or chocolate-covered walnuts or macadamias. Also look for glazed walnuts or glazed butter-toffee walnuts. And there are always honey-roasted peanuts, almonds, or cashews, not to mention vanilla-roasted nuts.

chocolate garnishes

chocolate leaves

Use only nontoxic unsprayed leaves, such as lemon leaves. Melt 3 ounces semisweet chocolate chips with 2 tablespoons vegetable shortening. Wash and dry 12 lemon leaves. With a pastry brush, spread a layer of melted chocolate on the back of each leaf. Place chocolate side up on a wax-paper-lined baking sheet, and refrigerate until firm, about 30 minutes. With cool hands, separate the chocolate from the leaves.

chocolate curls

For a small amount of chocolate curls to use as a garnish, pull a sharp vegetable peeler across the edge of a piece of room-temperature chocolate. Use any type—bittersweet, semisweet, milk, or white chocolate. For more volume, like the dessert on the cover, try chocolate shavings.

chocolate shavings

When you need more than just a few chocolate curls made with a vegetable peeler, try this method.

Melt chocolate chips or finely chopped bittersweet or semisweet chocolate in a heatproof bowl set over simmering water, stirring until smooth. With a large spatula, spread the chocolate as thinly as possible on a baking sheet. (A rimless baking sheet is ideal, but not necessary.) Refrigerate until the chocolate is set.

Remove the baking sheet from the refrigerator and let stand at room temperature for a few minutes. Using a sharp, wide metal spatula held at a 45-degree angle, scrape off a strip of chocolate; the chocolate will curl as it is scraped. (If the chocolate crumbles, let it warm up a little more.) Chill or freeze the curls until firm, or until ready to use.

what are cocoa nibs?

Cocoa nibs are roasted husked cocoa beans, broken into small bits. The basis for all types of chocolate, they have the most intense chocolate flavor of any substance. You can use them as a garnish as is or coarsely ground or ground to a powder (using a spice grinder). Made by Scharffen Berger, they are available in specialty food stores and many supermarkets, and from www.scharffenberger.com.

praline and praline powder

Although this is traditionally made with almonds, you can use your favorite nuts, or even coconut or pumpkin seeds. Either whole or chopped nuts are fine. If you are going to make the praline into a powder, it's best to use skinned or peeled nuts. I like to use a Polder probe thermometer when making praline—you can set the alarm to go off when the sugar mixture reaches the correct temperature, and it's not ungainly in the pan, like most candy thermometers. Or you can judge by the color.

makes about 12 ounces

1 cup chopped toasted hazelnuts or other nuts
¾ cup sugar
¼ cup light corn syrup

1. Generously butter a large baking pan. Spread the hazelnuts in the pan in a single layer.
2. Heat the sugar, ⅓ cup water, and the corn syrup in a large heavy saucepan over medium heat, stirring until the sugar is dissolved. Increase the heat to high and bring to a boil, washing down the sides of the pan with a damp pastry brush if you see any sugar crystals on the sides. Boil, without stirring, until the caramel turns a dark golden brown and registers 320 to 330 degrees F on a candy thermometer, continuing to wash down the sides of the pan with the pastry brush if necessary.

3. Immediately remove the saucepan from the heat and cautiously pour the caramel over the hazelnuts. Using an oiled heatproof rubber or metal spatula, spread the praline into as thin a layer as possible. Let stand at room temperature until set.

4. Break the praline into pieces, or transfer to a heavy plastic bag and crush with a rolling pin. Or pulse in a food processor to ¼-inch pieces, then process until the praline is pulverized to a powder.

. . . .

toasting nuts

Toasting nuts brings out or intensifies their flavor and helps prevent them from getting soggy if they will be submerged in a liquid. Preheat the oven to 350 degrees F. Spread the nuts in a single layer on a baking sheet. Toast, shaking the pan occasionally, for about 10 minutes, or until they are lightly browned and fragrant. Let cool before chopping.

To skin hazelnuts, toast them a little longer than other nuts, until the skins begin to pull away from the nuts. Then immediately wrap the nuts in a kitchen towel and let stand for 10 minutes. Rub the nuts in the towel to remove as much skin as possible; not all of it will come off, but that's okay.

. . . .

toasted marshmallows

Use a grill, a gas burner, or a campfire to toast these. Add whole strawberries or slices of banana to the skewers with the marshmallows for even more fun. Use as a garnish for sundaes, parfaits, and splits. If using bamboo skewers, soak them in water for 30 minutes first.

makes 4 skewers

12 marshmallows

Thread 3 marshmallows onto each of 4 skewers. Toast over an open flame until dark golden brown, or to desired doneness.

Garnishes Especially for Kids

Small-sized treats make the best garnishes for child-sized desserts. Here are some ideas to use on their own or in combination: chocolate sprinkles (jimmies), gumdrops, fireballs, Tootsie Rolls, Bit O'Honey, Reese's Pieces, Hot Tamales, Mike & Ike, Good & Plenty, gumballs, Jujubes, circus peanuts, candy hearts, Swedish berries or red fish, lollipops, gummy bears, red hot cinnamon candies, Lifesavers, M&M's, tiny candy-coated gum, Milk Duds, chocolate Kisses and Hugs, miniature marshmallows, caramel popcorn, Oreos, Teddy Grahams, wisps of cotton candy, Sugar Babies and Sugar Daddies, Tootsie Pops, jelly beans, or licorice twists, pipes, whips, and wheels.

You might also try orange and other fruit slices, or sliced fruit roll-ups. And, of course, animal crackers make a perfect kids' garnish.

Cookie Garnishes

From the most sophisticated pastry shop creations to store-bought cookies fondly remembered from childhood, cookies of all sorts make great garnishes for ice cream desserts. Here are some to try: gaufrettes (the classic French accompaniment to ice cream), whole or crumbled almond or coconut macaroons, paper-thin Moravian cookies, Mallomars, ginger or lemon snaps, pirouettes, chocolate wafers, graham crackers and chocolate graham crackers, shortbread, pecan sandies, biscotti, meringues, fortune cookies, palmiers, or chocolate chip cookies.

Garnishes for Ice Cream Drinks

For grown-ups, dip the rims of the serving glasses in water, rose water, a liqueur or spirit, or fruit juice and then into finely ground citrus zest mixed with sugar, finely ground crystallized ginger mixed with sugar, store-bought colored or flavored sugar, or granulated sugar stirred with just a pinch of spice (try nutmeg). Or use sifted unsweetened cocoa powder, or cocoa powder mixed with Ghirardelli sweet ground chocolate, or with instant espresso powder.

For kids (of all ages), dip the rims of serving glasses in melted chocolate and finely ground nuts, or in chocolate and then finely crushed peppermint or other hard candies.

- *Flooding a Plate*

Use wide-rimmed plates so the sauce has a barrier and doesn't run over the sides of the plate. Spoon the sauce into the center and tap the plate or tilt it to spread the sauce evenly.

- *Napping or Coating*

Spoon the sauce over the ice cream, letting it flow over and coat it.

- *Swirl*

Spoon sauces of two different flavors and colors, such as white and dark chocolate or raspberry and apricot, onto the plate, one on each half. Tilt the plate gently, first in one direction, then in the other, to swirl the edges of the sauces together.

. . . .

squeeze bottles and paintbrushes

Like an uptown restaurant pastry chef, fill squeeze bottles with your favorite sauces and use to garnish almost any dessert. The best effect is achieved using restraint. You can also use paintbrushes or pastry brushes to brush sauces on a plate, in any design, before adding the ice cream. Again, keep it simple.

. . . .

- *Teardrops*

Cover the bottom of serving plates with a dark sauce, such as raspberry or chocolate. Pipe or spoon small dots of a lighter-colored sauce or liquid, like white chocolate sauce or heavy cream, around the edge of the dark sauce. Gently pull a wooden pick through the dots to form teardrops. (It sounds complicated, but it isn't. Once you do one dot, you'll be a pro, and your dessert plates will look like it.)

- ### *Zigzags*
Arrange scoops of ice cream (or sorbet) on serving plates and pipe, squeeze, or spoon zigzag lines of a chilled sauce across the ice cream and plate. Dust with either sifted confectioners' sugar or cocoa, depending on the color and flavor of the ice cream, if desired.

- ### *Feathering*
Cover the bottom of a plate with a dark sauce, such as chocolate or caramel. Using a squeeze bottle, squeeze a dot of heavy cream or melted white chocolate onto the center of the plate, then squeeze one or several circles or a spiral around the center dot, working out from the center. Draw a wooden pick or skewer in straight lines from the center dot out to the rim of the plate through the sauce, like the spokes of a wheel.

- ### *Plate Border*
Using a squeeze bottle, squeeze swirls of chocolate, raspberry, strawberry, or other sauce around the edge of a serving plate to make a border. If desired, flood the center of the design with a sauce of a contrasting color.

- ### *Decorative Plate Squiggles*
Cover the bottom of a flat serving plate with a dark sauce such as chocolate or butterscotch. Using a squeeze bottle, squeeze squiggles of cream or a pale sauce over the first sauce.

THE

Scoop

1

SCOOP Dreams: CLASSIC COUPES, SUNDAES, PARFAITS, AND SPLITS

● ● ● ● ● ● ● ●

Coupe *means "cup" in French—like the Champagne coupe, the old-* fashioned shallow bowl-shaped glass. Ice cream coupes are more European in concept than our bigger-than-life all-American sundaes. They are essentially a very simple sundae— an ice cream or other frozen dessert and a topping served in a bowl or footed dish. The general rule is one or two scoops of ice cream with two to four tablespoons of a sauce, fruit mixture, or other topping. The possibilities are endless—mix and match any of the multitudes of store-bought or homemade sauces with any frozen dessert—and follow your bliss. Beginning on the next page, you'll find some suggestions for classic coupes made with liqueurs and spirits.

classic coupes

Anything goes. You can, with great results, use any flavor ice cream and any topping or sauce here. What sounds good? If you're not feeling particularly inspired, flip to page 35.

serves 4

1 to 2 pints vanilla ice cream
½ to 1 cup Warm or Cool Chocolate Sauce (page 175), Serious Chocolate Sauce (page 176), or store-bought chocolate sauce
Slightly Sweetened Whipped Cream (page 209), optional
4 ripe cherries or strawberries on the stem, optional

Place 1 or 2 scoops of the ice cream in each of four serving dishes. Top each dessert with 2 to 4 tablespoons of the sauce. Add a dollop of the whipped cream and garnish with the cherries, if using. Serve immediately.

GeLaTO aFFOGaTO

This classic Italian coupe is proof that cooking is alchemy. Something magic happens when you pour hot espresso over cold ice cream, and the play of warm against cold is irresistible. Affogato means "drowned" in Italian; the gelato is drowned in espresso—you'll be drowned in pleasure.

serves 2

1 pint vanilla gelato or ice cream
½ cup hot espresso or very strong brewed coffee
2 tablespoons Cognac or other brandy, optional

Place scoops of the gelato in four chilled short glasses or bowls. Pour the hot espresso, then the Cognac, if using, over the gelato, and serve immediately.

FLavor inspirations

Ice cream, frozen yogurt, gelato, and sorbet: Instead of vanilla, try cappuccino or espresso, chocolate, hazelnut, caramel, almond, tiramisù, chocolate or vanilla fudge swirl, mocha, licorice, or White Russian ice cream. Or try chocolate sorbet.

Spirits and liqueur: Instead of Cognac, try a dash of coffee, hazelnut, chocolate, almond, or anise liqueur; rum; or grappa.

Not necessary, but dazzling and divine: Garnish with chocolate curls (see page xxxviii), crushed Praline (page xxxix), a sparse dusting of cocoa powder or *very* finely ground coffee, chocolate-coated coffee beans, or a tiny dollop of Slightly Sweetened Whipped Cream (page 209). Serve with meringue cookies or chocolate-dipped citrus peel.

Ice cream coupes with liqueurs or spirits couldn't be easier, more grown-up, or more pleasurable. Serve these very sophisticated, very French desserts in bowls, glasses, or Champagne coupes. Follow these guidelines, or check out the "Flavor Inspirations" following the recipe.

Chilling or freezing the liqueur or spirit before assembling the desserts seems to add a certain *je ne sais quoi*, especially with sorbets. You needn't use a lot of liqueur. Either add just a splash, or arrange the scoops in serving dishes, make an indentation in the top of each one, and fill each indentation with a bit of liqueur.

In the spirit of keeping it simple, these recipes are proof that as long as you have ice cream in the freezer, you can put together a spectacular dessert in minutes—or less.

COUPES WITH amaretto

Especially here, less is more. You want just a hint of the liqueur. As for a simple garnish, here finely ground amaretti would be lovely.

serves 4

1 to 2 pints vanilla ice cream
¼ to ½ cup amaretto

Place 1 or 2 scoops of the ice cream in each of four serving dishes or glasses. Drizzle with the amaretto and serve immediately.

FLAVOR INSPIRATIONS
for ice cream coupes with liqueur

Vanilla ice cream with cranberry liqueur, with coffee liqueur and a dusting of instant espresso powder, with pear liqueur and chocolate curls (see page xxxviii) and/or cocoa nibs (see page xxxix), or with crème de cassis and mixed fresh berries

Chocolate ice cream with orange liqueur and chopped candied orange peel and/or crystallized ginger, with dark rum and toasted coconut, or with peppermint liqueur

Or chocolate ice cream, gelato, and/or sorbet with chocolate mint, coffee, maraschino, clementine, coconut, blackberry, or orange liqueur, or Chartreuse

Strawberry ice cream with crème de framboise or crème de cassis

Coffee or espresso ice cream with Cognac and toasted almonds

Peach ice cream with amaretto and crushed amaretti

Vanilla and orange swirl ice cream with orange liqueur

White chocolate ice cream with crème de noyaux (almond) and toasted slivered almonds

Apple pie ice cream and/or apple cider sorbet with Calvados

Macadamia brittle ice cream with macadamia liqueur

Ginger crème brûlée ice cream with ginger liqueur, or ginger gelato with ginger liqueur and finely ground gingersnaps or long thin strips of crystallized ginger

Mint gelato with chocolate mint liqueur

Espresso gelato with coffee liqueur, or anisette (think Sambuca with coffee beans), or White Russian gelato with coffee liqueur

Mango gelato with ginger liqueur

Honey gelato or ice cream with Drambuie

Coconut gelato, with or without mango gelato,
with coconut-flavored rum

Rose petal gelato with fraise de bois eau-de-vie

Fromage blanc gelato or sorbet with crème
de cassis or passion fruit, blueberry,
blackberry, or sour apple liqueur

Lemon sorbet with anisette, or lemon ice
cream and/or sorbet with lemon liqueur
(or a French "Colonel," lemon sorbet with
a splash of vodka)

Blackberry-lime sorbet with blackberry brandy,
or raspberry-cassis sorbet with crème de
cassis

Melon sorbet with a splash of Midori

Lemongrass sorbet with lemon liqueur

Lemon or coconut sorbet with lychee liqueur

Pink grapefruit sorbet with tequila and fresh
pomegranate seeds

Green apple sorbet with sour apple liqueur, or
with Calvados, garnished with a twist of
green apple peel

CHOCOLATE-DIPPED SPOONS

*Use dark, milk, or white chocolate, or lightly
dip two or three times into different ones,
forming layers. If you like, sprinkle the spoons
with about 3 tablespoons finely chopped nuts
before the chocolate sets. Serve alongside
coupes, sundaes, Gelato Affogato (page 6), or
Hot Ice Cream Sodas (page 49).*

MAKES 8 SPOONS

**2 ounces bittersweet or semisweet chocolate,
finely chopped**

1 teaspoon flavorless vegetable oil

1.   Cover a baking sheet with wax paper.

2.   Melt the chocolate with the oil in a heatproof
bowl set over a saucepan of simmering water, stirring until smooth.

3.   Dip the bowls and about ½ inch of the handles
of eight teaspoons or demitasse spoons in the
chocolate until coated, tilting the bowl of chocolate
and spooning the chocolate over the handles if necessary. Tap the spoons against the side of the bowl
to remove any excess chocolate. Lay the spoons on
the wax paper and let stand until the chocolate sets,
about 30 minutes.

Sundaes generally use at least two scoops of ice cream with three to four tablespoons of sauce or fruit topping. The sauce and the ice cream are often layered, usually topped with whipped cream and maybe a cherry or strawberry, and often garnished with a treat like nuts or candies. I don't use maraschino cherries on my sundaes, because I find them too sweet—just thinking about them makes my teeth ring—but if you love them, do use them.

With any of these concoctions, the balance of sauce to frozen dessert is important—like milk to cereal in the morning. You don't want all the sauce to be gone before the ice cream is, but you don't need a big puddle of the sauce in the dish when you're finished with the ice cream either. Also, too much of a very sweet sauce can overwhelm everything. Be careful to use sauces that aren't killer-sweet to your palate, and experiment with how much sauce you use on the ice cream. Be flexible with the recipes that follow; sometimes the amount of ice cream or topping will depend a great deal on the dishes or glasses you're using. The amounts of topping I call for may be slightly too much for your dishes, but I doubt if it will ever be too little.

Make your own sauces and toppings using the recipes in the sauce chapter or buy them in the supermarket or at specialty food stores (or even on the Internet). Fruit syrups are also great drizzled over frozen desserts, and there is a wide variety of these available as well. Some are pure concentrated fruit with no added sugar; these are generally available in health food stores and some supermarkets. Also consider pancake-style fruit-flavored syrups available in supermarkets, specialty food stores, and online. If you enjoy maple syrup on your ice cream, be sure to use the real thing—and note that because it's darker and less refined, Grade B syrup actually has more flavor than Grade A.

Take advantage of the many recipes for flavored whipped cream on pages 209–210, and add a dollop of chocolate, cherry, caramel, or another whipped cream to your desserts. Use real cream in a can with a nozzle if you'd rather not whip your own.

Want to flambé your sundaes? Soak 1 sugar cube per sundae in a spirit of at least 70 percent alcohol. Place the cubes on top of the sundaes, light them with a match, and take the sundaes to the table—carefully—while they are still flaming.

Scooping isn't the only way to a sundae or split. You can also remove a pint of solidly frozen ice cream from the container with a small metal spatula or table knife, and slice it crosswise into rounds or vertically into wedges. These rounds or wedges can be tightly wrapped and frozen until just before serving. Or put the pint on a serving plate, leaving the ice cream in one piece, top with a sauce, decorate the "tower" with berries or other fruit, and cut into wedges to serve.

LIVE-IT-UP HOT FUDGE SUNDAES

Although no one knows for certain the derivation of the word sundae, *it's often credited to the owner of a Midwestern soda fountain in the 1800s. The story is that at the time the favorite ice cream delight was an ice cream soda, but blue laws prohibited the consumption of carbonated beverages on Sunday. So he topped ice cream with a syrup to create a "dry" soda, which he called a* sundae, *rather than* Sunday, *so as not to be sacrilegious. But that didn't stop a hot fudge sundae from being a religious experience. The hot fudge sundae was first served at C. C. Brown's in Hollywood.*

serves 4

¾ cup **Easiest Hot Fudge Sauce (page 173),**
    Old-fashioned Hot Fudge Sauce (page 174),
    or store-bought hot fudge sauce, warmed
2 pints **vanilla ice cream**
Slightly Sweetened Whipped Cream (page 209)
    or one of the variations
¼ cup **toasted sliced almonds**
4 **fresh cherries or strawberries on the stem**

1. Spoon 1 tablespoon of the fudge sauce into each of four sundae dishes. Add 1 scoop of the ice cream to each, then top with another tablespoon of fudge sauce. Repeat with one more scoop of ice cream and another tablespoon of sauce in each dish.

2. Add a dollop of the whipped cream to each sundae, garnish with the almonds and cherries, and serve immediately.

FLAVOR
INSPIRATIONS

Ice cream, frozen yogurt, and gelato: Instead of vanilla, try chocolate, coffee, coconut, hazel-nut, tiramisù, lemon, peanut butter fudge, peach, caramel, ginger, cinnamon, orange, cookies and cream, almond praline, peppermint, triple caramel chunk, turtle sundae, cherry vanilla, pistachio, or white chocolate.

Nuts: Instead of almonds, use chopped or whole toasted Brazil nuts, hazelnuts, pecans, peanuts, cashews, pine nuts, pistachios, pumpkin seeds, macadamias, or walnuts.

Not necessary, but dazzling and divine: Along with or instead of the almonds, add candied chestnuts; fresh ripe berries; sliced peaches, bananas, apricots, or figs; broiled pineapple wedges; small canned pear halves; crumbled meringues, amaretti, or graham crackers; miniature marsh-mallows; M&M's; crushed peanut brittle or peppermint candies; chopped crystallized ginger; toasted coconut; sprinkles or dragées; a dusting of instant espresso powder; a splash of amaretto or another liqueur or spirit; and/or blazing sparklers.

HOT caramel sundaes

Caramel is my favorite culinary trick. Melting and browning sugar gives it a much more complex flavor; it turns plain old one-dimensional sweet into irresistible bittersweet. Warm caramel sauce over cold ice cream is one of the world's very few absolutely perfect combinations.

serves 4

¾ cup Old-fashioned Caramel Sauce (page 181), or one of the variations, or store-bought caramel sauce, warmed

2 pints vanilla ice cream

Slightly Sweetened Whipped Cream (page 209) or Caramel Whipped Cream (page 210)

¼ cup toasted cashews, optional

1. Spoon 1 tablespoon of the caramel sauce into each of four sundae dishes. Add 1 scoop of the ice cream to each, then top with another tablespoon of caramel sauce. Repeat with one more scoop of the ice cream and another tablespoon of the sauce in each dish.

2. Add a dollop of the whipped cream to each sundae, garnish with the cashews, if using, and serve immediately.

FLAVOR INSPIRATIONS

Ice cream, frozen yogurt, and gelato: Instead of vanilla, try caramel cashew crunch, butter brickle, chocolate caramel swirl, vanilla caramel brownie, apple crumble, macadamia brittle, coffee toffee, pralines and cream, cinnamon caramel, nutty waffle cone, Heath bar crunch, peanut turtles, or crème caramel pecan.

Nuts: Instead of cashews, use chopped or whole toasted Brazil nuts, hazelnuts, almonds, peanuts, pecans, pine nuts, pistachios, pumpkin seeds, macadamias, or walnuts.

Not necessary, but dazzling and divine: Along with or instead of the cashews, garnish with Poached Pears (page 26) or canned pears, sliced fresh peaches, or plums; large or small pieces of Praline (page xxxix) or brittle; a tiny drizzle of chocolate or hot fudge sauce; or fresh blueberries.

HOT BUTTERSCOTCH SUNDAES

The best butterscotch always has some salt in it to balance the sweetness. If your store-bought version doesn't, add just a pinch. Or, if you prefer, another way to balance the sweetness is to add a squeeze of fresh lemon juice.

serves 4

¾ cup Scottish-Style Butterscotch Sauce (page 183) or store-bought butterscotch sauce, warmed
2 pints vanilla ice cream
Slightly Sweetened Whipped Cream (page 209) or Butterscotch Whipped Cream (page 210)
¼ cup chopped toasted hazelnuts, optional

1.   Spoon 1 tablespoon of the butterscotch sauce into each of four sundae dishes. Add 1 scoop of the ice cream to each, then top with another tablespoon of butterscotch sauce. Repeat with one more scoop of ice cream and another tablespoon of the sauce in each dish.

2.   Add a dollop of the whipped cream to each sundae, garnish with the hazelnuts, if using, and serve immediately.

FLAVOR INSPIRATIONS

Ice cream, frozen yogurt, and gelato: Instead of vanilla, try toasted hazelnut crunch, apple crumble, ginger, coffee, peach, apple cream pie, bananas Foster, cinnamon, macadamia brittle, pecan pie, coconut, or dulce de leche.

Nuts: Instead of hazelnuts, use chopped or whole toasted Brazil nuts, almonds, peanuts, cashews, pine nuts, pistachios, pumpkin seeds, macadamias, or walnuts.

Not necessary, but dazzling and divine: Along with or instead of the hazelnuts, add chopped or ground hard caramel, Praline (page xxxix), molasses chips, toffee, or brittle; miniature butterscotch chips and miniature chocolate chips; or chopped nougat. Serve with pirouette cookies.

She was a butterscotch sundae of a woman.

✳

—A. J. LIEBLING, *ON LILLIAN RUSSELL*

DUSTY MILLER SUNDAES

Growing up in California, I never heard of a Dusty Miller—it's an East Coast thing. I learned all about them from my great friend and fellow foodie Jennifer Wehrle. They were her favorite childhood pleasure at the Palm Beach Bath and Tennis Club. The word on the street is that they may have originated at the Jupiter Island Club in Hobe Sound, Florida. Pass a small bowl of the malted milk powder at the table.

serves 4

¾ cup Warm or Cool Chocolate Sauce (page 175),
Lighter Chocolate Sauce (page 176),
or store-bought chocolate sauce
2 pints vanilla ice cream
¼ to ½ cup chocolate-flavored malted milk
powder
Slightly Sweetened Whipped Cream (page 209)
or Chocolate Malt Whipped Cream
(page 210), optional

1. Spoon 1 tablespoon of the chocolate sauce into each of four sundae dishes. Add 1 scoop of the ice cream to each, then top with another tablespoon of chocolate sauce. Repeat with one more scoop of ice cream and another tablespoon of sauce in each dish.

2. Dust the sundaes with the malted milk powder. Add a dollop of the whipped cream to each sundae, if using, and serve immediately.

FLAVOR INSPIRATIONS

Ice cream, frozen yogurt, and gelato: Instead of vanilla, try malted milk ball, milk chocolate, chocolate, coffee, caramel, chocolate fudge swirl, vanilla fudge, or coffee fudge.

Not necessary, but dazzling and divine: Garnish with whole or chopped malted milk balls.

BLACK-AND-TAN SUNDAES

A classic that is unlikely to ever lose its appeal—try one, and you'll see why.

serves 4

⅓ cup Old-fashioned Caramel Sauce (page 181)
   or store-bought caramel sauce, warmed
⅓ cup Warm Chocolate Sauce (page 175)
   or store-bought chocolate sauce, warmed
2 pints vanilla ice cream
Slightly Sweetened Whipped Cream (page 209),
   Caramel Whipped Cream (page 210),
   or Chocolate Whipped Cream (page 210)
Toasted whole pecans, optional

1. Spoon 1 tablespoon of each of the sauces into each of four shallow serving dishes, placing them next to each other. Place 1 scoop of the ice cream on each spoonful of sauce. Top each scoop with another spoonful of each sauce.

2. Add a dollop of the whipped cream to each scoop, garnish with the pecans, if using, and serve immediately.

FLAVOR INSPIRATIONS

Ice cream, frozen yogurt, and gelato: Instead of vanilla, try caramel and chocolate, amaretto crunch, Louisiana praline, chocolate caramel, caramel praline crunch, vanilla with chocolate and caramel, triple caramel chunk, caramel fudge decadence, English toffee, vanilla caramel pecan, dark chocolate and pecan, tin lizzie sundae, tin roof sundae, turtle sundae, or vanilla caramel brownie.

Nuts: Instead of pecans, try chopped or whole toasted Brazil nuts, hazelnuts, almonds, peanuts, toasted coconut, cashews, pine nuts, pistachios, pumpkin seeds, macadamias, or walnuts.

Not necessary, but dazzling and divine: Garnish with Praline (page xxxix), crumbled cookies, chopped chocolate-covered toffee, chocolate leaves (see page xxxviii), cocoa nibs (see page xxxix), molasses chips, or sliced ripe peaches, cherries, or plums.

have a make-your-own-ice-cream-sundae party

Set out sundae dishes, spoons, scoops, a big bowl of Slightly Sweetened Whipped Cream (page 209), and lots of sauces and syrups and ice creams. Consider a warm caramel sauce, a chocolate sauce, Sliced Strawberry Topping (page 188) or Strawberries Romanoff (page 148), and maybe Easiest Marshmallow Sauce (page 185). Or, if you'd rather be a little less traditional, offer an all-tropical theme with tropical fruit ice cream, sorbets, and sauces. Choose whatever you love and think your guests will enjoy.

TIN LIZZIE SUNDAES

Never had one? The sooner you have your first, the sooner you can have your second. Vanilla is classic, but use any ice cream flavor you like.

serves 4

⅓ cup Old-fashioned Caramel Sauce (page 181)
   or store-bought caramel sauce, warmed
⅓ cup Warm Chocolate Sauce (page 175)
   or store-bought chocolate sauce, warmed
2 pints vanilla ice cream
Slightly Sweetened Whipped Cream (page 209),
   Caramel Whipped Cream (page 210),
   or Chocolate Whipped Cream (page 210)
Chocolate-covered peanuts for garnish

1.　Spoon 1 tablespoon of each of the sauces into each of four sundae dishes. Place 1 scoop of the ice cream in each dish, then top with 1 tablespoon of each sauce. Repeat with one more scoop of ice cream and another spoonful of each sauce in each dish.

2.　Add a dollop of the whipped cream to each sundae, garnish with the chocolate-covered peanuts, and serve immediately.

TIN ROOF SUNDAES

The classic "Tin Roof" is two scoops of vanilla side by side, not piled on top of each other, in a shallow bowl, with red-skinned peanuts covering the ice cream and forming the rusty tin roof. You can use any flavor ice cream you hanker for. You can add whipped cream, but I think this is better without—and I don't say that about many things.

serves 4

1 cup Warm or Cool Chocolate Sauce (page 175)
    or store-bought chocolate sauce
2 pints vanilla ice cream
Lightly salted red-skinned peanuts

1. Spoon 2 tablespoons of the chocolate sauce next to each other on each of four shallow serving dishes. Place 1 scoop of the ice cream on each spoonful of sauce. Top each scoop with 1 tablespoon of the sauce.

2. Cover the top of the sundaes with the peanuts and serve immediately.

It is illegal to carry ice cream in your back pocket in Kentucky.

*

Black-and-White Sundaes

For this dessert, it's best to use a wide, shallow dish, because you want to show off the contrasting colors of the ice creams and sauces.

⅓ cup Easiest Marshmallow Sauce (page 185)
⅓ cup Cool Chocolate Sauce (page 175),
   Chocolate Marshmallow Sauce (page 178),
   or store-bought chocolate sauce
1 pint chocolate ice cream
1 pint vanilla ice cream
Slightly Sweetened Whipped Cream (page 209)
   or Chocolate Whipped Cream (page 210)

1. Spoon 1 tablespoon of each of the sauces next to each other on each of four shallow serving dishes. Place a scoop of the chocolate ice cream on the marshmallow sauce and a scoop of the vanilla on the chocolate sauce. Top each scoop of chocolate ice cream with a spoonful of marshmallow sauce and each scoop of vanilla with a spoonful of chocolate sauce.

2. Add a dollop of the whipped cream to each scoop and serve immediately.

FLAVOR INSPIRATIONS

Ice cream, frozen yogurt, and gelato: Instead of chocolate and vanilla, try chocolate mint, tiramisù, banana split, candy bar sundae, coffee, chocolate marshmallow, fudge ripple, rocky road, vanilla and chocolate swirl, cookies and cream, cherry vanilla fudge, or peanut butter marshmallow, in any combination.

Not necessary, but dazzling and divine: Garnish with Toasted Marshmallows (page xl) on skewers, fresh fruit or grilled strawberries on skewers, grilled or broiled bananas, a drizzle of raspberry syrup, or meringue cookies.

bananas foster

Bananas Foster originally came from Brennan's Restaurant in New Orleans, where it's still served as a finale to their famous brunch. Be careful not to overcook the bananas; you want them to be just softened, not mushy, and they should still hold their shape. I like to substitute 1 tablespoon, more or less, of dark muscovado sugar (or dark brown sugar) for about a tablespoon of the light brown sugar. The muscovado sugar adds a toffee flavor with no extra work or cooking. A staple in English kitchens, muscovado sugar is available in specialty food stores.

serves 4

4 tablespoons (½ stick) unsalted butter
½ cup packed light brown sugar
1 teaspoon fresh lemon juice
3 medium bananas, peeled, halved crosswise on
    the diagonal, and halved lengthwise
2 tablespoons dark rum or brandy
1 to 2 pints vanilla ice cream

1. Combine the butter, sugar, and lemon juice in a large nonstick skillet over medium heat, stirring until the sugar is dissolved. Arrange the bananas in the skillet and cook, shaking the pan and gently turning the bananas once, for 2 minutes, or until they are browned and beginning to soften. Add the rum and heat the mixture. Carefully tip the pan slightly to ignite the rum, or light it with a long match. When the flames subside, carefully transfer the bananas to four serving plates.

2. Add scoops of the ice cream next to the bananas. Spoon the warm sauce over the bananas and ice cream, and serve immediately.

FLAVOR INSPIRATIONS

Ice cream, frozen yogurt, and gelato: Instead of vanilla, try butter pecan, banana, dulce de leche, ginger, butter brickle, bananas Foster, honey almond, macadamia brittle, banana fudge chunk, banana Heath bar crunch, caramel, or banana walnut praline.

Not necessary, but dazzling and divine: Substitute 8 spears of ripe pineapple for the bananas and garnish with chopped macadamia nuts.

cherries jubilee

Cherries Jubilee was named for Queen Victoria's Diamond Jubilee, and it's a great dish for a celebration—although it's easy enough to make on a school night. Hot and cold together is a remarkable treat, and this may be the original fire-and-ice dessert.

serves 4

2 tablespoons unsalted butter

12 ounces (2 cups) ripe Bing cherries, stemmed and pitted

2 tablespoons light brown sugar

2 tablespoons kirsch or brandy

1 to 2 pints vanilla ice cream

1. Melt the butter in a large nonstick skillet over medium heat. Add the cherries and sugar and cook, stirring, for 5 minutes, or until the sugar is dissolved and the cherries are beginning to soften.

2. Add the kirsch and heat the mixture. Carefully tip the pan slightly to ignite the kirsch, or light it with a long match. When the flames subside, carefully transfer the cherries to four bowls or serving plates.

3. Add scoops of the ice cream. Spoon some of the warm sauce over the cherries and ice cream, and serve immediately.

FLAVOR INSPIRATIONS

Ice cream, frozen yogurt, gelato, and sorbet: Instead of vanilla, try almond, caramel, lemon, peach, white chocolate, pistachio, chocolate, orange and vanilla swirl, ginger, cherry vanilla, German chocolate cake, vanilla fudge, vanilla raspberry swirl, chocolate cherry cordial, cheesecake, black forest, or try vanilla ice cream and peach, chocolate, or cherry sorbet.

Not necessary, but dazzling and divine: At the table, carefully spoon the cherries over the ice cream while the sauce is still flaming.

peach melba

The combination of peaches, vanilla ice cream, and raspberry sauce was created by Auguste Escoffier in the late 1800s to honor Dame Nellie Melba, "The Australian Nightingale." The carved ice swan he served it in is not necessary, but the pistachios I've suggested make a great garnish. Peach Cardinal is very much like Peach Melba, but it uses strawberry ice cream and red currant jelly instead of the raspberry sauce.

Feel free to use 8 drained canned peach halves (from a 29-ounce can) instead of the poached peaches, if you prefer; toss them gently with 2 teaspoons fresh lemon juice and ¼ teaspoon pure vanilla extract before using. Another option is to transfer the poached peaches to a bowl, add the raspberry sauce, and refrigerate, tightly covered, for at least 2 and up to 8 hours, until the peaches absorb the flavor and color of the sauce.

serves 4

4 firm but ripe small peaches
⅔ cup sugar
Grated zest and juice of 1 lemon
1 teaspoon pure vanilla extract

1 to 2 pints vanilla ice cream
Raspberry Sauce (page 187) or store-bought
  raspberry sauce
Finely ground pistachios, optional

1. Immerse the peaches in a large pot of boiling water for 45 seconds. Remove them with a slotted spoon. Slip off the peels, cut the peaches in half, and remove the pits.

2. Bring 2 cups water, the sugar, lemon zest and juice, and vanilla to a boil in a large saucepan over high heat, stirring until the sugar is dissolved. Add the peach halves and return the mixture to a boil, then reduce the heat to low, and simmer for 4 to 5 minutes, or until the peaches are easily pierced with a fork. With a slotted spoon, transfer the peaches to a plate, and let cool; set the syrup aside. Use the peaches immediately, or return to the syrup when cooled, and refrigerate, tightly covered, for up to 3 days before draining and serving chilled.

3. Place 2 peach halves, cut side up, in each of four serving bowls or plates. Arrange scoops of the ice cream on the side, drizzle both peaches and ice cream with 1 to 2 tablespoons of the sauce, and garnish with the pistachios, if using. Serve immediately, and pass additional sauce at the table, if desired.

Ice cream, frozen yogurt, gelato, and sorbet: Instead of vanilla, try peach, raspberry, ginger, caramel, rose petal, strawberry, white chocolate or vanilla with raspberry swirl, blackberry, blueberry, cassis, pistachio, or peach Melba. Or try a combination of vanilla ice cream and raspberry or peach sorbet, peach ice cream and peach sorbet, or raspberry ice cream and raspberry sorbet.

Not necessary, but dazzling and divine: Place a few raspberries or almonds in the center of each peach half. Garnish with candy-coated fennel seeds, chocolate-coated raspberries, fresh cherries on the stem, crushed Praline (page xxxix), Jordan almonds, fresh (unsprayed edible) or crystallized flowers, or minced crystallized ginger. Serve with shortbread or meringue cookies.

· ·

the original *pêche melba*

Inspired by a performance of *Lohengrin,* in which Madame Melba took the role of Elsa, Escoffier created a new sweet as a surprise for the brilliant singer, who was dining at [London's] Savoy [Hotel restaurant] the following day. Peaches and vanilla ice cream were served on a silver dish set between the wings of a swan, recalling the famous scene from the opera; this swan was carved from a block of ice and covered with *sucre filé* (spun sugar). The sweet was named *Les Pêches au Cygne.*

The necessity of carving the swan out of ice, using hot irons, chisels, and knives, prevented the sweet from becoming generally popular. It was not until some eight years later, on 1 July 1899, to celebrate the opening of the Carlton Hotel in London's Haymarket, that Escoffier added the raspberry puree to this recipe and told a waiter to set it before Melba. She enjoyed it so much she asked its name and Escoffier sent back a request. "Would she allow him to call it *Pêches Melba?*" Thus was created the true *Pêche Melba.*

—Caroline Liddell and Robin Weir, *Ices: The Definitive Guide*

· ·

pears belle hélène

The dish is classically served on rounds of sponge cake, but I don't think you need go to the trouble. You can use canned pear halves for a very quick dessert (a 29-ounce can will contain at least 8 pear halves), or poach your own (see the instructions following the recipe). In either case, handle the pears gently, as they are delicate. Sprinkle the dessert with ground Praline (page xxxix) after adding the chocolate sauce, if desired. It's also wonderful with the tiniest drizzle of Old-fashioned Caramel Sauce (page 181) or Caramel Syrup (page 199) in addition to the chocolate sauce.

serves 4

8 canned pear halves or poached pear halves
(recipe follows), drained
¼ teaspoon pure vanilla extract
1 to 2 pints vanilla ice cream
Warm Chocolate Sauce (page 175), Serious
Chocolate Sauce (page 176), or store-
bought chocolate sauce, warmed
4 candied violets, optional

1. Gently toss the pear halves with the vanilla in a bowl.

2. Place pear halves, cut side up, in each of four serving bowls or plates. Arrange scoops of the ice cream on the side, drizzle 1 to 2 tablespoons of the chocolate sauce over the ice cream and pears, and garnish with the violets, if using. Serve immediately, and pass additional sauce at the table, if desired.

poached pears

Bring 2 cups water, ⅔ cup sugar, the zest of 1 lemon removed with a vegetable peeler, the juice of that same lemon, and 1 teaspoon pure vanilla extract to a boil in a large saucepan over high heat, stirring until the sugar is dissolved. Add 4 peeled, halved, and cored pears and return to the boil, then reduce the heat and simmer gently, stirring occasionally, for 5 to 7 minutes, or until the pears are easily pierced with a fork. With a slotted spoon, transfer the pears to a plate, and let cool slightly; set the syrup aside. Use the pears immediately, or return to the syrup when cooled and refrigerate, tightly covered, for up to 1 week before draining and serving chilled.

Ice cream, frozen yogurt, gelato, and sorbet: Instead of vanilla, try cinnamon, chocolate and vanilla, butter pecan, pralines and cream, toasted almond, cheesecake, vanilla fudge swirl, ginger, white chocolate, pistachio, or caramel. Or try pear and ginger sorbet and vanilla ice cream.

Not necessary, but dazzling and divine: Instead of the violets, garnish with chocolate leaves or curls (see page xxxviii), Microwave Chocolate-Dipped Strawberries (page 116), crystallized ginger, candied lemon or orange peel, ground gingersnaps or cocoa nibs (see page xxxix), chocolate truffles, crushed Praline (page xxxix), finely ground pistachios, or honey roasted almonds. Or serve with gingersnaps.

A hot fudge sundae and a trashy novel is my idea of heaven.

*

— BARBARA WALTERS

café LIÈGEOIS

Liège, a city in Belgium, is credited with originating this chic French classic. In Parisian cafés it is often garnished with candied violets—use them instead of the optional coffee beans if you happen to have some in the cupboard. Adjust the amount of sugar added to the coffee to suit your taste—you might not want to add any at all. If you are short on time, quickly chill the coffee by putting it in a large glass measure, placing that in a shorter bowl of ice and water, and stirring or whisking the coffee occasionally, adding fresh ice as the ice melts, until the coffee is chilled. (Make sure no ice water gets into the coffee.) Serve with pirouette cookies, if you like.

serves 4

1½ cups hot strong brewed coffee
1 tablespoon sugar, or to taste
1 to 2 pints coffee ice cream
Slightly Sweetened Whipped Cream (page 209)
     or one of the variations
4 coffee beans, optional

1. Stir together the coffee and sugar in a glass measure until the sugar is dissolved. Refrigerate, covered, until very cold, about 20 minutes.

2. Spoon 2 tablespoons of the coffee into each of four large stemmed dishes. Scoop the ice cream into the dishes and pour the remaining coffee over the top. Spoon a dollop of the whipped cream onto each sundae, garnish with the coffee beans, if using, and serve immediately.

variation

Chocolate Liègeois: Also a classic in Parisian cafés. Substitute 1½ cups hot chocolate for the coffee (omit the sugar) and chill it. Use chocolate ice cream, and garnish with chocolate curls (see page xxxviii), if desired.

ultimate Brownie sundaes

After a simple family dinner or a fancy dinner party, this dessert is an extraordinary delight. Whether you make the brownies or buy them, it's a good idea to keep some (hidden) in the freezer, for the next time you must thoroughly treat yourself.

serves 4

4 brownies
1 to 2 pints vanilla ice cream
Serious Chocolate Sauce (page 176),
    Milk Chocolate–Peanut Butter Sauce
    (page 179), Warm Chocolate Sauce (page 175),
    Chocolate Raspberry Sauce (page 177),
    or store-bought chocolate sauce, warmed
Slightly Sweetened Whipped Cream (page 209)
    or one of the variations
4 fresh strawberries on the stem, optional

Arrange the brownies on four serving plates. Top with scoops of the ice cream and drizzle with the chocolate sauce. Add a dollop of the whipped cream to each sundae, garnish with the strawberries, if using, and serve immediately.

Flavor Inspirations

Ice cream, frozen yogurt, and gelato: Instead of vanilla, try rocky road, black raspberry chip, coconut, ginger, malted milk ball, mocha chip, butter pecan, chocolate mint, chocolate hazelnut, peppermint crunch, tiramisù, chocolate raspberry truffle, chocolate peanut butter, cinnamon, coffee, coffee almond fudge, cherry vanilla, cookies and cream, chocolate marshmallow, turtle sundae, candy bar sundae, strawberry, or Neapolitan.

Nuts: Top with chopped or whole toasted Brazil nuts, almonds, hazelnuts, pecans, peanuts, cashews, pine nuts, pistachios, pumpkin seeds, macadamias, or walnuts; or chocolate-covered nuts or honey-roasted nuts.

Not necessary, but dazzling and divine: Garnish with Microwave Chocolate-Dipped Strawberries (page 116), cherries on the stem, strawberry fans (see page xxxv), mixed berries tossed with Caramel Syrup (page 199), chopped Praline (page xxxix) or peanut brittle, chocolate leaves or curls (see page xxxviii), Chocolate-Covered Bananas (page 157), crushed peppermint candies, chocolate-covered mints, toasted marshmallows, chocolate chips, or chocolate peanut butter chips.

Variation

Ultimate Gingerbread Sundaes: Substitute squares of gingerbread for the brownies.

Parfaits are essentially tall sundaes, with layers that you can see through the tall dishes or glasses that they are usually served in. Parfaits are all about the contrast of colors, textures, and flavors. The best parfaits, like the best sundaes and coupes, use ice creams and sauces in colors and flavors that complement each other rather than fight for attention. Consider layering ice cream or gelato with sorbet, a treat to eat and to look at, especially if layered with fruit or fruit sauces; try, for example, blueberry sorbet, vanilla ice cream, and orange sorbet with fresh blueberries and/or a blueberry sauce. To construct a parfait, spoon a bit of the sauce or fruit in first, then layer the ice cream and sorbet with the fruit until you reach the top. Use the sauces and toppings you would use for a sundae, and/or syrups or liqueurs, and add crumbled cookies, or whatever is at hand and sparks your imagination. A general rule of thumb is one or two tablespoons of sauce or topping between each of at least three layers of ice cream, but, again, there are no real mistakes here. Do top your parfaits with whipped cream, and a cherry or strawberry on the stem or a slice of fruit.

ice cream parfaits

You'll want to use tall slender dishes or glasses for the parfaits. For best results, chill them before filling.

serves 4

1 cup Cool Chocolate Sauce (page 175), Lighter
   Chocolate Sauce (page 176), or store-bought
   chocolate sauce
2 pints vanilla ice cream, slightly softened
Slightly Sweetened Whipped Cream (page 209)
4 fresh strawberries or cherries on the stem,
   optional

1.   Spoon 1 tablespoon of the chocolate sauce into each of four chilled parfait dishes. Add 1 scoop of the ice cream to each, then top each with another tablespoon of chocolate sauce. Repeat with two more scoops of the ice cream, with another tablespoon of the sauce over each scoop.

2.   Add a dollop of the whipped cream to each parfait, garnish with the strawberries, if using, and serve immediately.

variation

If you want clear and separate layers for your parfaits, start by placing the parfait dishes in the freezer for 15 minutes. Fill each one about one-third full with ice cream and smooth the top to make an even layer. Add about 1 tablespoon of the sauce to each dish and return the dishes to the freezer for 10 minutes. Add enough ice cream to each dish to fill it almost two-thirds full. Smooth the top to make an even layer and top each with another tablespoon of the sauce. Return the dishes to the freezer for 10 minutes. Finally, add enough ice cream to each dish to fill it almost to the top. Smooth the top into an even layer and top each with another tablespoon of sauce. Chill in the freezer for at least 10 minutes, or, tightly covered, up to 1 day. Top with whipped cream before serving.

Flavor inspirations

Ice cream, frozen yogurt, gelato, and sorbet: Mix and match ice creams, frozen yogurts, gelatos, and/or sorbets with sauces. Try fruit and berry frozen desserts with fruit and berry sauces; caramel and nut flavors with caramel sauces; chocolate and fruit flavors with chocolate and hot fudge sauces.
Not necessary, but dazzling and divine: Layer crushed candies between the layers. Praline (page xxxix) works with almost every flavor combination.

Banana splits are exciting, fun, and, for me, a meal in themselves. And for all their eye-widening impact, they are easy to make. First, arrange the split banana in the dish. I prefer to face the cut sides of the banana inward, although some who have been to official sundae school insist they should face out. Then add three scoops of ice cream: the traditional vanilla, strawberry, and chocolate isn't a hard-and-fast rule, especially if you prefer raspberry, mango, and coconut gelato and/or sorbet. Another tradition is to spoon chocolate sauce over the strawberry, strawberry sauce over the chocolate, and pineapple over the vanilla, but you can use any contrasting sauces you like. Generously dollop each scoop of ice cream with whipped cream, sprinkle with chopped toasted nuts, and top with a strawberry or cherry on the stem.

In short, make your banana splits any way you like. Or break with tradition and don't use bananas at all. Splits are great with mangoes, nectarines, peaches, apricots, pineapple, plums, melon, or papayas. Most of these fruits can be grilled or broiled; I wouldn't cook the papayas or the melon, but any of the others take to browning wonderfully well.

banana SPLITS

This formula, of course, is flexible. You might grill, broil, or roast the bananas, or sprinkle the cut bananas with granulated sugar and scorch with a kitchen propane torch until well caramelized. Or use tiny Mexican bananas or red bananas, or even Chocolate-Covered Bananas (page 157). But do brush the cut bananas with fresh lemon juice if you're not using them immediately to prevent them from discoloring. As a variation, you might want to use grilled or broiled wedges of pineapple instead of the bananas.

serves 4

4 bananas, peeled and halved lengthwise
1 pint vanilla ice cream
1 pint chocolate ice cream
1 pint strawberry ice cream
About ¼ cup Old-fashioned Caramel Sauce
    (page 181) or store-bought caramel sauce
About ¼ cup Cool Chocolate Sauce (page 175)
    or store-bought chocolate sauce
About ¼ cup Smooth Strawberry Sauce (page 188)
    or store-bought strawberry sauce
Slightly Sweetened Whipped Cream (page 209)
    or one of the variations

Toasted sliced almonds
12 small fresh strawberries or cherries on the
    stem, optional

1. Arrange 2 banana halves in each of four long narrow dessert dishes. Arrange 3 large scoops of the ice cream in a line between the banana halves in each dish, using 1 scoop of each flavor.

2. Top the vanilla ice cream with the caramel sauce, the chocolate with the chocolate sauce, and the strawberry with the strawberry sauce. Spoon a dollop of the whipped cream over each scoop of ice cream, sprinkle with the almonds, and garnish with the strawberries, if using. Serve immediately.

Ice cream, frozen yogurt, and gelato: Use any trio of ice cream, frozen yogurt, and/or gelato that calls to you. Try double chocolate chip, mocha chocolate chip, and peanut butter chocolate chip with chocolate and/or hot fudge sauces; black cherry, black raspberry, and blackberry with raspberry, blackberry, and cherry sauces; raspberry cheesecake, blueberry cheesecake, and strawberry cheesecake with raspberry, blueberry, and strawberry sauces; milk chocolate, dark chocolate, and white chocolate with dark chocolate, white chocolate, and cherry sauces; eggnog, pumpkin, and rum raisin with butter rum sauce; caramel, caramel apple, and cinnamon caramel with caramel sauce; coffee, tiramisù, and chocolate with chocolate sauce; peach, cherry, and apricot with cherry sauce; or pralines and cream, dulce de leche, and Heath bar crunch with chocolate sauce.

Sorbet: Use mango, coconut, and pineapple sorbet with fresh pineapple, fresh mango, and Passion Fruit Caramel Sauce (page 182); strawberry, raspberry, and blueberry with strawberry, raspberry, and blueberry sauces; lemon, orange, and lime with a tiny chocolate sauce drizzle, cherry sauce, or raspberry sauce; guava, guanabana, and piña colada with fresh fruit and coconut. Or try coconut sorbet, ice cream, and gelato with chocolate sauce.

FLAVOR INSPIRATIONS

for coupes, sundaes, parfaits, and splits

For elegant coupes, instant espresso powder sprinkled over coffee chocolate chip ice cream topped with chocolate sauce

Vanilla gelato coupes with a drizzle of artisanal balsamic vinegar (if you have only commercial balsamic, try Brown Sugar–Balsamic Sauce, page 150)

Apricot gelato coupes with chocolate sauce, sprinkled with toasted hazelnuts or almonds

Scoops of assorted brightly colored sorbets with White Chocolate Sauce (page 180), garnished with fresh fruit or berries

Cherry ice cream coupes with cherries steeped in brandy and a drizzle of chocolate sauce

Cheesecake ice cream coupes with Cherry Sauce (page 191) or Blueberry Sauce (page 185)

Green tea ice cream with Serious Chocolate Sauce (page 176), garnished with a tiny pinch of matcha green tea

At holiday time, chestnut ice cream with chocolate sauce (your choice) and a candied chestnut garnish

Warm orange marmalade thinned with a little orange liqueur over orange and vanilla ice cream, or over chocolate ice cream

Grand sundaes of chocolate sorbet, caramel ice cream, chocolate and/or caramel sauce, whipped cream, and crushed Praline (page xxxix)

For kids especially, chocolate ice cream sundaes with Easiest Marshmallow Sauce (page 185) and chocolate sprinkles; or cookies and cream ice cream topped with Easiest Marshmallow Sauce and crumbled chocolate sandwich cookies

For very quick and easy s'mores sundaes, chocolate sauce spooned over graham crackers, topped with scoops of chocolate ice cream, dolloped with Easiest Marshmallow Sauce (page 185), and garnished with Toasted Marshmallows (page xl), if you like

In the spring, strawberry ice cream with Smooth Strawberry Sauce (page 188) and sliced ripe apricots; later in the season, peach ice cream with Raspberry Sauce (page 187) and mixed fresh berries

Espresso ice cream or gelato with Easiest Hot Fudge Sauce (page 173), and biscotti on the side

Hazelnut praline ice cream with chocolate sauce, whipped cream, and big chunks of Praline (page xxxix) on top

Brownie sundaes with dulce de leche ice cream and Easiest Hot Fudge Sauce (page 173)

Pineapple-coconut ice cream with Scottish-Style Butterscotch Sauce (page 183) and macadamia nuts and/or toasted coconut

Caramel ice cream topped with orange segments tossed with Caramel Syrup (page 199)

Coffee ice cream, dark chocolate sauce, coffee liqueur, whipped cream, and chocolate shavings

Strawberry ice cream and sorbet with Raspberry Sauce (page 187) swirled with Easiest Marshmallow Sauce (page 185)

Lemon ice cream sundaes with Blueberry Sauce (page 185), topped with fresh raspberries and/or sliced ripe peaches, whipped cream, and toasted hazelnuts; or lemon or lime sorbet and vanilla ice cream sundaes or parfaits with Blackberry Sauce (page 187) or any berry sauce

Coconut ice cream sundaes with chocolate sauce, or any of the following with chocolate sauce: malted milk gelato, raspberry ice cream, lemon or orange ice cream, mint ice cream, ginger ice cream, vanilla ice cream and orange sorbet, pistachio ice cream, or cinnamon ice cream

Ginger ice cream with Passion Fruit Syrup (page 206), whipped cream, and minced crystallized ginger

Sundaes of peach or ginger ice cream, sauced with maple syrup heated with minced crystallized ginger, a bit of butter, and a pinch of finely grated lemon zest

Coffee ice cream topped with Warm Chocolate Sauce (page 175) and garnished with toasted sliced almonds

Peach ice cream with a splash of pure maple syrup and the tiniest dusting of finely ground gingersnaps

Orange sorbet and vanilla ice cream with Raspberry Sauce (page 187), garnished with quartered ripe black figs and, perhaps, a sprinkling of toasted pine nuts or pistachios

Chocolate peanut butter ice cream topped with Milk Chocolate–Peanut Butter Sauce (page 179) and crushed peanut brittle or dry-roasted peanuts

For a grown-up indulgence, chocolate ice cream topped with candied chestnuts, Serious Chocolate Sauce (page 176), julienned candied orange peel, and a splash of rum or Grand Marnier.

White chocolate ice cream with Cherry Sauce (page 191) or Dried Sour Cherry Sauce (page 191), or bittersweet chocolate sorbet with White Chocolate Sauce (page 180)

For a "Knickerbocker Glory," just like they serve at the Fortnum & Mason tearoom in London, sugared raspberries, crushed pineapple, and vanilla and strawberry ice cream layered in tall parfait glasses and topped with whipped cream and cherries

For over-the-top banana splits, Chocolate-Covered Bananas (page 157) with chocolate, coffee, and caramel gelato; chocolate, coffee, and caramel sauces; whipped cream; and crushed Praline (page xxxix)

Banana—or peach—splits with strawberry ice cream, drizzled with Raspberry Sauce (page 187), topped with whipped cream, and sprinkled with cocoa nibs (see page xxxix)

Vanilla, chocolate, and coffee ice creams topped, respectively, with Coffee Sauce (page 184), Raspberry Sauce (page 187), and the chocolate sauce of your choice, whipped cream, and fresh raspberries

2

CLASSIC FOUNTAIN DRINKS: A Parade of Sodas, Milkshakes, Freezes, Floats, and More

● ● ○ ○ ○ ○ ○ ○

Ice cream sodas are easy to make. Just take a small scoop of ice cream, stir it together (called "muddling" in soda fountain parlance) with flavored syrup in the bottom of a tall glass, add chilled carbonated water, then another larger scoop of ice cream, and top with whipped cream and a strawberry or cherry on the stem (or the garnish of your choice). But even though they are so easy to make, ice cream sodas are an out-of-the-ordinary thing, and a great way to put smiles on the faces of your family and friends without taking up much of your precious time.

Ice cream sodas are also very flexible. The decision of how much syrup to add is a personal one. I like big, intense flavors in these drinks, but if the syrup is overly sweet and you use a lot of it, the drink will be too sweet. The 3 tablespoons used in these recipes should make almost everyone very happy, but you might find you prefer a little more or a little less. This will also depend on the size glass you're using; if it's especially large, use a little more syrup and ice cream.

I recommend using seltzer. It's pure carbonated water, whereas club soda is carbonated water that contains mineral salts, such as sodium bicarbonate—which tampers with the flavor of the soda. It's been said that if you use seltzer from a siphon, you'll have a creamier drink, but I think that as long as you stir the syrup and ice cream together well before you add the carbonated water, the soda will be very creamy.

Use any of the flavored syrup recipes found on pages 198–208, or try the high-quality syrups widely available for sale. European syrups are very good; you should be able to find black currant, sour cherry, and strawberry in most supermarkets, and more flavors in specialty food stores. There are also some excellent American-made syrups—but don't use the ones that are intended for flavoring coffee.

I often use fruit nectars and juices to make sodas. You need to use more of them than of a syrup, because their flavor isn't as concentrated, but they work very well. Consider guava, passion fruit, mango, guanabana, pineapple, black cherry, papaya, blueberry, pomegranate, peach, apricot, or pear. The intensely flavorful juices from the health food store are perfect for sodas; my favorite is Montmorency cherry juice. Use between ¼ and ½ cup juice or nectar per soda, and be sure to chill it well before beginning.

When you're serving ice cream sodas to grown-ups, consider using a liqueur instead of or with the syrup. You can have a lot of fun matching the liqueur flavor with the ice cream, gelato, or frozen yogurt.

Top your creations with Slightly Sweetened Whipped Cream (page 209) or one of the flavored variations. (These all make enough whipped cream to serve 4 people.) Or use real cream in a can with a nozzle, if you'd like; Isigny Ste.-Mère makes a good one. You can also use an immersion blender to whip up just a small amount of cream; sweeten it to your taste.

Tips for Making Ice Cream Sodas

- If you will be serving several people, you can scoop the ice cream ahead of time. Place the scoops on a wax-paper-lined chilled plate, cover tightly, and store in the freezer until you're ready to prepare the drinks.
- Make sure all of the ingredients you use are very cold, as well as the glasses.
- Most of all, be certain to serve the sodas while they are still fizzing.

Black-and-White ice cream soda

The combination of chocolate syrup and vanilla ice cream in a soda is a time-honored treat from the days when soda fountains were the social center of many communities. This popular dessert still makes any occasion memorable.

serves 1

3 tablespoons Chocolate Syrup (page 198)
   or store-bought chocolate syrup
1 cup vanilla ice cream
Chilled carbonated water, preferably seltzer
Slightly Sweetened Whipped Cream (page 209),
   optional
A fresh strawberry or cherry on the stem, optional

1. Pour the syrup into a tall glass. Add about ¼ cup of the ice cream, and stir until well combined. Pour enough of the carbonated water into the glass to fill it about half-full, then add the remaining ice cream and, if there is any room left, more carbonated water. Top the soda with a dollop of the whipped cream and the strawberry, if using.

2. Place the glass on a saucer or small plate and serve immediately, with a straw and a long-handled spoon.

Brown Cow Ice Cream Soda

Although most ice cream sodas are made with plain carbonated water, this one is made with root beer. It resembles a root beer float—with the addition of chocolate syrup.

serves 1

3 tablespoons Chocolate Syrup (page 198)
   or store-bought chocolate syrup
1 cup vanilla ice cream
Chilled root beer
Slightly Sweetened Whipped Cream (page 209),
   optional

1. Pour the syrup into a tall glass. Add about ¼ cup of the ice cream, and stir until well combined. Pour enough of the root beer into the glass to fill it about half-full, then add the remaining ice cream and, if there is any room left, more root beer. Top the soda with a dollop of the whipped cream, if using.
2. Place the glass on a saucer or small plate and serve immediately, with a straw and a long-handled spoon.

variation

Black Cow Soda: Use cola instead of root beer.

Always serve too much hot fudge sauce on hot fudge sundaes. It makes people overjoyed, and puts them in your debt.

*

—JUDITH OLNEY

chocolate ice cream soda

For the true chocolate lover, this makes an ideal dessert any time of the year. It's also a perfect afternoon pick-me-up. For a dessert, you might add a little rum, brandy, Grand Marnier, or crème de cacao. For a mocha soda, use all or part coffee ice cream.

serves 1

3 tablespoons Chocolate Syrup (page 198)
    or store-bought chocolate syrup
1 cup chocolate ice cream
Chilled carbonated water, preferably seltzer
Slightly Sweetened Whipped Cream (page 209)
    or Chocolate Whipped Cream (page 210),
    optional
Unsweetened cocoa powder for dusting, optional

1. Pour the syrup into a tall glass. Add about ¼ cup of the ice cream, and stir until well combined. Pour enough of the carbonated water into the glass to fill it about half-full, then add the remaining ice cream and, if there is any room left, more carbonated water. Top the soda with a dollop of the whipped cream and a light sifting of cocoa powder, if using.

2. Place the glass on a saucer or small plate and serve immediately, with a straw and a long-handled spoon.

coffee ice cream soda

Coffee-and-ice-cream drinks are among my favorite things. There are a couple of others in The Scoop: Café Liègeois (page 28), which is chilled coffee and coffee ice cream, and Hot Ice Cream Soda (page 49), which is hot coffee and vanilla ice cream. This is the only fizzy one, and it is scrumptious.

serves 1

3 tablespoons Coffee Syrup (page 200)
   or store-bought coffee syrup
1 cup coffee ice cream
Chilled carbonated water, preferably seltzer
Slightly Sweetened Whipped Cream (page 209)
   or Coffee Whipped Cream (page 210),
   optional
1 chocolate-covered coffee bean, optional

1.   Pour the syrup into a tall glass. Add about ¼ cup of the ice cream, and stir until well combined. Pour enough of the carbonated water into the glass to fill it about half-full, then add the remaining ice cream and, if there is any room left, more carbonated water. Top the soda with a dollop of the whipped cream and the chocolate-covered coffee bean, if using.

2.   Place the glass on a saucer or small plate and serve immediately, with a straw and a long-handled spoon.

Watching other teams in the World Series is like watching someone else eat a hot fudge sundae.

*

—JOE TORRE,
MANAGER, NEW YORK YANKEES

BUTTERSCOTCH or caramel ice cream soda

A simple and elegant treat. You might think about using caramel ice cream with the caramel sauce.

serves 1

3 tablespoons Scottish-Style Butterscotch Sauce (page 183), Old-fashioned Caramel Sauce (page 181), or store-bought butterscotch or caramel sauce
1 cup vanilla ice cream
Chilled carbonated water, preferably seltzer
Slightly Sweetened Whipped Cream (page 209) or Caramel or Butterscotch Whipped Cream (page 210), optional
A chunk of Praline (page xxxix) or peanut brittle, optional

1. Pour the sauce into a tall glass. Add about ¼ cup of the ice cream, and stir until well combined. Pour enough of the carbonated water into the glass to fill it about half-full, then add the remaining ice cream and, if there is any room left, more carbonated water. Top the soda with a dollop of the whipped cream and the praline, if using.

2. Place the glass on a saucer or small plate and serve immediately, with a straw and a long-handled spoon.

THE Broadway ice cream soda

Named after the famous New York City thoroughfare, this is a quintessential NYC drink—two stimulants in one glass.

serves 1

3 tablespoons Chocolate Syrup (page 198)
   or store-bought chocolate syrup
1 cup coffee ice cream
Chilled carbonated water, preferably seltzer
Slightly Sweetened Whipped Cream (page 209)
   or Mocha Whipped Cream (page 210),
   optional

1. Pour the syrup into a tall glass. Add about ¼ cup of the ice cream, and stir until well combined. Pour enough of the carbonated water into the glass to fill it about half-full, then add the remaining ice cream and, if there is any room left, more carbonated water. Top the soda with a dollop of the whipped cream, if using.

2. Place the glass on a saucer or small plate and serve immediately, with a straw and a long-handled spoon.

Without ice cream, there would be darkness and chaos.

*

—DON KARDONG, *1976*
OLYMPIC MARATHONER

strawberry ice cream soda

Pink and frothy, there's something very feminine about a strawberry soda.

serves 1

3 tablespoons Strawberry Syrup (page 200)
   or store-bought strawberry syrup
1 cup strawberry ice cream
Chilled carbonated water, preferably seltzer
Slightly Sweetened Whipped Cream (page 209)
   or Strawberry Whipped Cream (page 209),
   optional
A fresh strawberry on the stem, optional

1.   Pour the syrup into a tall glass. Add about ¼ cup of the ice cream, and stir until well combined. Pour enough of the carbonated water into the glass to fill it about half-full, then add the remaining ice cream and, if there is any room left, more carbonated water. Top the soda with a dollop of the whipped cream and the strawberry, if using.

2.   Place the glass on a saucer or small plate and serve immediately, with a straw and a long-handled spoon.

FLAVOR INSPIRATIONS

Syrup: Instead of strawberry, try any fruit or berry syrup, such as cherry, raspberry, blackberry, nectarine, plum, lemon, peach, apricot, or orange. Or use a fruit or berry liqueur.

Ice cream, gelato, and frozen yogurt: Instead of strawberry, try mixing and matching other flavors, depending on the syrup. Or replace some of the ice cream with sorbet for a more powerful flavor.

have your own ice-cream-soda party

Arrange ice cream scoops, ice cream soda glasses, long-handled spoons, napkins, and straws on the table. Have chilled syrups such as chocolate, strawberry, or whatever flavors you prefer at the ready, along with plenty of chilled seltzer. At the last minute, bring out an assortment of ice creams—consider vanilla, chocolate, strawberry, and coffee. Don't forget the whipped cream.

HOT ICE CREAM SODA

Believe it or not, in the 1960s, hot ice cream sodas were served at H. Hicks of Manhattan, which boasted of selling more than two thousand different ice cream concoctions. H. Hicks gave the recipe to food editor Clementine Paddleford, who ran it in the New York Herald Tribune. *This is an adaptation of a formula I found in Paul Dickson's* Great American Ice Cream Book. *Strictly speaking, it's not a soda, but it's a delicious surprise.*

serves 1

2 tablespoons unsweetened cocoa powder
1 tablespoon sugar, or to taste
1 cup hot strong brewed coffee
1 cup vanilla ice cream
Slightly Sweetened Whipped Cream (page 209), optional

1. Put the cocoa and sugar in a blender. Pour in half the hot coffee and blend until smooth. Add the remaining coffee.

2. Scoop the ice cream into a tall glass and add a long-handled spoon (this prevents the glass from cracking). Pour the coffee mixture over the ice cream. As soon as the ice cream floats to the top, add a dollop of the whipped cream, if using, and serve.

I used to fear ice cream would be the ruin of me, but I gave up giving it up a long time ago.

*

—BEATRICE LILLIE

Milkshakes are the *soda fountain classic. If you're nostalgic for the good old* days, when you got the milkshake left in the mixing container served alongside the glass, you can re-create the experience at home—easily. And, if you like really thick milkshakes, it's best to make them at home.

When soda fountains were at the height of their popularity, nobody had blenders or a milkshake machine in the kitchen. A milkshake was an exceptional treat, and certainly not something you could make at home.

Your definition of what a milkshake is will depend mostly on where you grew up. Imagine my surprise, as a California native, when I moved to Boston and discovered a "milkshake" there was flavored milk that was shaken up—no ice cream at all. If I wanted what I knew as a milkshake, with ice cream in it, I had to order a frappé. All of the following milkshakes contain ice cream.

The general formula for a milkshake that serves two is 1 pint of ice cream, about ¼ cup flavored syrup, and ½ to ¾ cup milk, well combined in a milkshake machine or blender. I usually use the lesser amount of milk because I like a very thick milkshake. In fact, I prefer a shake that's so thick it has large pieces of ice cream in it, so I don't blend until smooth. Each of these recipes makes about 2 cups, for 2 people, so I suggest you use shorter, wider glasses rather than really tall ones.

Be creative. Use the following recipes as guidelines, and use one of the myriad syrups and your latest favorite exotic ice cream flavor. Add seasonal fresh fruits if you like, mixing and matching them with the ice cream flavors, and maybe even some sorbet.

Tips for Making Milkshakes

- Use really cold milk.
- Chill the glasses in the freezer so they'll be frosty cold.
- Don't overblend; overmixing will make the milkshake thin.
- If you like a really thick milkshake, wait to add some of the ice cream
  until after you've poured the drink into the glass.

quadruple-chocolate milkshakes

It's perfectly fine to make this with regular milk and slightly sweetened whipped cream, but maybe with the chocolate milk and the chocolate whipped cream you'll finally feel you have sufficient chocolate in your diet.

serves 2

¼ cup Chocolate Syrup (page 198)
    or store-bought chocolate syrup
½ to ¾ cup chilled chocolate milk or milk
1 pint chocolate ice cream
Chocolate Whipped Cream (page 210) or Slightly
    Sweetened Whipped Cream (page 209),
    optional

1. Pour the syrup into a blender. Add the milk and blend until smooth. Add half of the ice cream and blend just until thick. Add the remaining ice cream and blend just to combine.

2. Pour the milkshakes into two chilled glasses. Top with dollops of the whipped cream, if using, and serve immediately, with straws and spoons.

FLAVOR INSPIRATIONS

Syrup and sauce: Instead of chocolate, try Coffee Syrup (page 200), Caramel Syrup (page 199), Easiest Marshmallow Sauce (page 185), Cherry Syrup (page 204), Toasted Coconut Syrup (page 207), Peach Syrup (page 203), Orange Syrup (page 205), or Ginger Syrup (page 207) and adjust the ice cream flavor accordingly.

Ice cream, frozen yogurt, gelato, and sorbet: Instead of or along with the chocolate, try coffee, hazelnut, coconut, banana fudge, chocolate caramel, cinnamon, vanilla fudge twirl, pistachio, or mocha almond fudge. Or use part raspberry or chocolate sorbet.

Not necessary, but dazzling and divine: Add 2 tablespoons creamy peanut butter, Nutella or other hazelnut chocolate spread; rum; or orange, hazelnut, coffee, chocolate, or raspberry liqueur. Add sliced fresh peaches, bananas, or berries, or a dusting of cinnamon or nutmeg. Or garnish with cherries or strawberries on the stem.

chocolate malted milkshakes

These are terrific with whole or chopped malted milk balls as a garnish. I prefer Ovaltine over Carnation brand malted milk powder; I grew up with it, and I had the coolest aluminum Ovaltine shaker, just like a martini shaker.

serves 2

¼ cup Chocolate Syrup (page 198)
   or store-bought chocolate syrup
½ to ¾ cup chilled milk or chocolate milk
¼ cup chocolate-flavored malted milk powder,
   plus (optional) more for garnish
1 pint chocolate ice cream
Slightly Sweetened Whipped Cream (page 209) or
   Chocolate Malt Whipped Cream (page 210),
   optional

1. Pour the syrup into a blender. Add the milk and malted milk powder and blend until smooth. Add half of the ice cream and blend just until thick. Add the remaining ice cream and blend just to combine.
2. Pour the milkshakes into two chilled glasses. Top with dollops of the whipped cream and a dusting of malted milk powder, if using, and serve immediately, with straws and spoons.

coffee milkshakes

We coffee addicts know who we are. We love the flavor as much as the jolt. You might also add 2 tablespoons or so of coffee liqueur.

serves 2

¼ cup Coffee Syrup (page 200) or store-bought
  coffee syrup
½ to ¾ cup chilled milk
1 pint coffee ice cream
Slightly Sweetened Whipped Cream (page 209)
  or Coffee Whipped Cream (page 210),
  optional

1. Pour the syrup into a blender. Add the milk and blend until smooth. Add half of the ice cream and blend just until thick. Add the remaining ice cream and blend just to combine.

2. Pour the milkshakes into two chilled glasses. Top with dollops of the whipped cream, if using, and serve immediately, with straws and spoons.

strawberry milkshakes

Strawberry's dandy, but you can use any fruit-flavored syrup with any berry or other fruit ice cream—just mix and match.

serves 2

¼ cup Strawberry Syrup (page 200)
    or store-bought strawberry syrup
½ to ¾ cup chilled milk
1 pint strawberry ice cream
Slightly Sweetened Whipped Cream (page 209)
    or Strawberry Whipped Cream (page 209),
    optional
2 ripe fresh strawberries on the stem, optional

1.   Pour the syrup into a blender. Add the milk and blend until smooth. Add half of the ice cream and blend just until thick. Add the remaining ice cream and blend just to combine.

2.   Pour the milkshakes into two chilled glasses. Top with dollops of the whipped cream and the strawberries, if using, and serve immediately, with straws and spoons.

liqueur milkshakes

Follow the recipe for any one of the milkshakes, using liqueur along with or instead of the syrup. You'll need 2 to 4 tablespoons of liqueur per serving, but be careful not to make the shakes too sweet.

Chocolate Syrup (page 198) and chocolate cheesecake, chocolate raspberry truffle, hazelnut, chocolate peanut butter, or cherry ice cream, or tiramisù gelato

Raspberry Syrup (page 202) and chocolate or peach ice cream

Orange Syrup (page 205) and raspberry ice cream, or orange and vanilla swirl ice cream

Strawberry Syrup (page 200) and mango ice cream, rose petal gelato, or strawberry shortcake ice cream

Toasted Coconut Syrup (page 207) and pineapple ice cream

Caramel Syrup (page 199) and Heath bar crunch, butter pecan, dulce de leche, cinnamon, macadamia brittle, or apple pie ice cream

Blueberry Syrup (page 201) and blueberry cheesecake ice cream

Blackberry Syrup (page 202) and ginger ice cream

Peach Syrup (page 203) and peaches and cream or peach Melba ice cream

Mango Syrup (page 206) and mango, passion fruit, coconut, and/or pineapple ice cream

Ginger Syrup (page 207) and ginger or ginger crème brûlée ice cream

Lemon Syrup (page 204) and lemon gelato

Passion Fruit Syrup (page 206), or any tropical fruit syrup, and vanilla gelato

Coffee Syrup (page 200) and chocolate gelato

Caramel Syrup (page 199) and caramel ice cream with a brittle or Praline (page xxxix) garnish

Ginger Syrup (page 207) and ginger ice cream with a crystallized ginger garnish

Toasted Coconut Syrup (page 207) and coconut ice cream or gelato with a toasted coconut garnish

Milkshakes and sodas are magnificent, but freezes are my favorite fountain drink (today, anyway). A freeze is fairly flexible—it's made with sorbet rather than ice cream, and either carbonated water or fruit juice or nectar. I think of it as simply a soda prepared without syrup, although you could toss in some syrup too, if you wanted to. Freezes are terrifically refreshing.

These are not tall drinks, so use shorter glasses, and chill them before filling.

For liqueur freezes, add liqueurs to freezes in addition to the juice or nectar; use 2 to 4 tablespoons per serving.

peach freeze

Using this recipe as a guideline, mix and match your favorite juices and nectars with your favorite sorbets. Many of the nectars available in cans these days are calcium fortified, so if you use them, the freeze will be quite healthful.

serves 2

1 cup chilled peach juice or nectar
1 pint peach sorbet
Juice of 1 lemon

1. Pour the peach juice into a blender. Add the sorbet and 2 tablespoons lemon juice and blend until almost smooth but still very thick. Add more lemon juice to taste, if desired.

2. Pour into two chilled glasses and serve immediately, with straws and spoons.

FLAVOR INSPIRATIONS

Juice and nectar: Instead of peach juice, try mango, apricot, guava, guanabana, piña colada, or passion fruit juice or nectar; lemonade or limeade; or flavored orange juice, such as orange and strawberry.

Sorbet: Instead of peach, try mango, strawberry, raspberry, lemon, passion fruit, tangerine, orange, ginger lemon, cassis, guanabana, cherry, coconut, lemongrass, apricot, piña colada, or lime.

Ice cream, frozen yogurt, and gelato: Replace half (or less) of the sorbet with vanilla, strawberry, coconut, pineapple, mango, or orange and vanilla swirl ice cream.

Not necessary, but dazzling and divine: Add a dash of orange liqueur or orange-flower water. Coat the rims of the glasses with colored sugar before filling, or garnish with fruit on a skewer or with tiny paper umbrellas.

CHOCOLATE Freeze

Here's a freeze that uses carbonated water rather than juice or nectar. It's very refreshing, and the flavor possibilities are endless.

serves 2

1 cup chilled carbonated water, preferably seltzer
1 pint chocolate sorbet

1. Pour the carbonated water into a blender. Add the sorbet and blend until almost smooth but still very thick.
2. Pour into two chilled glasses and serve immediately, with straws and spoons.

FLAVOr
INSPIraTIONS

Sorbet: Instead of chocolate, try blackberry, grapefruit, apricot, cosmopolitan, coconut, blueberry, or green apple.

Not necessary, but dazzling and divine: Garnish with chocolate leaves or curls (see page xxxviii), cocoa nibs (see page xxxix), or a sprinkling of instant espresso powder or ground sweet chocolate.

Floats are similar to ice cream sodas, but they do not include syrup and are simply made with flavored bubbly water and ice cream. Just stir together a bit of the soda and some of the ice cream, then add more soda and top with the rest of the ice cream. Remember, you can make a float out of whatever you want—because you're a grown-up. Mrs. Colton, my third-grade teacher, invited my whole class to her house one Saturday afternoon, and we each made our own ice cream sodas. She really impressed me by using Coke and chocolate ice cream for her float.

A 12-ounce can of soda should be more than enough for any of these floats.

For liqueur or spirit floats, add about 2 tablespoons of your favorite liqueur or spirit to any of the ice cream floats.

root beer float

My enduring favorite. Probably yours too. Use ice-cold mugs like the carhops used to serve at A&W. In my hometown, they still do—on roller skates.

serves 1

Chilled root beer
1 cup vanilla ice cream

1. Pour about ¼ cup of the root beer into a tall chilled glass. Add about ¼ cup of the ice cream and stir to combine. Slowly pour enough root beer into the glass to fill it about half-full, then add the remaining ice cream and, if there is any room left, more root beer.

2. Serve immediately, with a straw and a long-handled spoon.

FLAVOR
INSPIRATIONS

Soda: Instead of root beer, use any cola; Cel-Ray, cream soda, birch beer, or sarsaparilla; black cherry, orange, lemon-lime, pineapple, coconut, tamarind, limonata, raspberry-lime rickey, bitter lemon, apple, grapefruit, cassis, watermelon, Key lime, peach, or coffee soda; ginger ale or flavored ginger ale; or Moxie, Ting, Dr Pepper, Orangina, Squirt, or Fresca.

Belch Water: Glass of seltzer

Black Stick: Chocolate ice cream cone

Bucket: Large scoop

Burn: Malted milkshake, generally chocolate

City Juice: Water

Drop: Sundae

Glob: Plain sundae

Hoboken Special: Pineapple sundae with chocolate ice cream

House Boat: Banana split

L.A.: À la mode

Nervous Pudding: Jell-O

Sand: Sugar

Suds: Root beer

White Cow: Vanilla milkshake

—Paul Dickson's *Great American Ice Cream Book*

GInGer Beer FLOaT

In my opinion, the hotter the ginger beer, the better. My favorite float is made with Reed's Ginger Beer and Ciao Bella's Tahitian vanilla gelato. This recipe also tastes great with coconut or mango ice cream.

serves 1

Chilled ginger beer
1 cup vanilla ice cream

1. Pour about ¼ cup of the ginger beer into a tall chilled glass. Add about ¼ cup of the ice cream and stir to combine. Slowly pour enough ginger beer into the glass to fill it about half-full, then add the remaining ice cream and, if there is any room left, more ginger beer.

2. Serve immediately, with a straw and a long-handled spoon.

Ice cream is exquisite.
What a pity it isn't illegal.

*

—VOLTAIRE (FRANÇOIS MARIE AROUET,
1694–1778), FRENCH PHILOSOPHER

STRAWBERRY BLONDE FLOAT

Another classic from days gone by. You could use some strawberry sorbet with the strawberry ice cream for an even more intense flavor. Or be daring and use raspberry ice cream instead—or more daring and use mango, coconut, coconut-pineapple, blueberry, ginger, or peach. You'll have to make up your own names for those floats!

serves 1

Chilled ginger ale
1 cup strawberry ice cream
A fresh strawberry on the stem, optional

1. Pour about ¼ cup of the ginger ale into a tall chilled glass. Add about ¼ cup of the ice cream and stir to combine. Slowly pour enough ginger ale into the glass to fill it about half-full, then add the remaining ice cream and, if there is any room left, more ginger ale. Garnish with the strawberry, if using.

2. Serve immediately, with a straw and a long-handled spoon.

PURPLE COW FLOAT

I've never met a child who would turn down a Purple Cow.

serves 1

Chilled grape soda
1 cup vanilla ice cream

1. Pour about ¼ cup of the grape soda into a tall chilled glass. Add about ¼ cup of the ice cream and stir to combine. Slowly pour enough grape soda into the glass to fill it about half-full, then add the remaining ice cream and, if there is any room left, more grape soda.
2. Serve immediately, with a straw and a long-handled spoon.

We dare not trust our wit for making our house pleasant to our friend, and so we buy ice-creams.

*

— RALPH WALDO EMERSON
(1803–82), AUTHOR, POET,
AND PHILOSOPHER

LeMOnaDe 'n' SORBeT

For even more pizzazz, add fresh fruit and/or berries. Sliced strawberries, whole raspberries or blueberries, and sliced or diced apricots, nectarines, plums, or peaches are all great. Serve with a long-handled spoon. Use lots of sorbet or just a little. You can use up to a pint to serve 4, but just 3 tiny scoops in each glass also looks great.

Use the "quick-chill" method following the recipe, if you're in a hurry. Or buy the lemonade and just add sorbet. Lorina brand sparkling lemonade from France is brilliant— try the plain, pink, or berry lemonade.

serves 4

1 cup sugar
Pinch of salt
1 whole lemon, thinly sliced, or the zest of 1 lemon
   removed with a vegetable peeler
1 cup fresh lemon juice (from about 4 large
   lemons)
1 to 2 cups lemon sorbet

1. Bring 3½ cups water, the sugar, and the salt to a boil in a large saucepan over high heat, stirring until the sugar is dissolved. Remove from the heat, add the sliced lemon, and let stand, covered, for 10 minutes.

2. Pour the syrup into a pitcher or glass measure, straining it, if desired. Stir in the lemon juice. Refrigerate, covered, until very cold.

3. Partially fill four chilled glasses with the lemonade. Scoop large or small balls of the sorbet and add to the glasses. Serve immediately.

quick chill

Place the lemonade in a large glass measure and place it in a bowl that's shorter than the measure. Add ice and water to the bowl and chill the lemonade, stirring or whisking occasionally, and adding fresh ice and water as the ice melts. Just be sure that the ice water doesn't get into the lemonade.

Sorbet: Instead of lemon, try watermelon, passion fruit, peach, pear, guava, lemongrass, Meyer lemon, tangerine, pineapple, green apple, grapefruit, ginger lemon, blueberry, cassis, apricot, blood orange, raspberry, strawberry, mango, cherry, blackberry, orange, or lime.

Variations: Sweeten your lemonade with Caramel Syrup (page 199) instead of the sugar. Or use sparkling cider or flavored cider instead of the lemonade. For a liqueur Lemonade 'n' Sorbet, stir any liqueur or spirit into the lemonade before adding the sorbet. Use ½ to 1½ ounces per serving.

sgroppino

This isn't a classic all-American soda fountain dessert at all, but it might become one at your house. It is a classical close to a meal throughout the Veneto region of Italy, where it's served all year round as a palate cleanser just before dessert. It's almost always made with lemon sorbetto there. Prosecco, a bright, clean, and slightly fruity wine from the Veneto, is available as both a sparkling and a still wine, but it's the sparkling version that is best here.

serves 4

1½ cups chilled prosecco, Champagne, or
   other sparkling wine
1 pint lemon sorbet
¼ cup vodka, optional

1. Pour the prosecco into a blender. Add the sorbet and the vodka, if using, and blend just until smooth but still thick.
2. Pour into chilled glasses and serve immediately, with spoons.

FLAVOR
INSPIRATIONS

Sorbet: Instead of lemon, try cassis, raspberry, mango, coconut, orange, peach, strawberry, passion fruit, grapefruit, green apple, or pineapple.

Ice cream, frozen yogurt, and gelato: Replace all or half of the sorbet with vanilla, lemon, peach, raspberry, mango, or strawberry.

Spirits: Instead of vodka, try flavored vodka, grappa, limoncello, or an eau-de-vie.

Not necessary, but dazzling and divine: Add sliced ripe fresh fruit, such as peaches or berries, a fruit sauce, or a fruit syrup, and blend before adding the sorbet. Garnish with tiny champagne grapes.

sorbet and champagne

Sorbet in a glass of Champagne is something almost no one would turn down. The combination is a natural, and you can use any sparkling wine, not just Champagne. Probably the most famous Champagne drink is a Kir Royale, made with Champagne and crème de cassis. Why not change that to Champagne with a scoop of cassis sorbet? Here are some other ideas:

- A Mimosa, orange sorbet with Champagne, perhaps with a drop of orange-flower water
- Champagne sorbet with Champagne
- Peach sorbet with Rosé Champagne, garnished with a slender peach wedge
- Wild strawberry sorbet with Champagne
- Blood orange sorbet with Champagne and a twist of orange peel
- Cherry sorbet and Champagne, garnished with a cherry
- Mango sorbet and Champagne, with a strip of fresh mango
- Grapefruit sorbet and Champagne

You might also try ginger, lemon, raspberry, green apple, lemon verbena, lemongrass, melon, or peach sorbet with your favorite sparking wine.

Here's a general formula for making these cocktails:

1. Freeze Champagne flutes.
2. Scoop tablespoon-sized balls of sorbet—one for each glass—and freeze them on a wax-paper-lined plate, covered, for up to several hours before serving.
3. To serve, transfer the scoops of sorbet to the glasses. Slowly fill the glasses with Champagne. Stir once, if desired, and add a twist of citrus peel, if you'd like.

- Make a White Russian with vanilla ice cream instead of heavy cream.
- Try a Lemon Drop cocktail with a small scoop of lemon or lemongrass sorbet.
- Add vanilla or coffee ice cream to an Irish coffee instead of the whipped cream. (Or use both.)
- Add chocolate ice cream or sorbet to a Brandy Alexander or a Grasshopper.

3

Frosty Pies, Chilly Cakes, and Baked Alaska:
Pies, Cakes, and Meringues

● ● ● ○ ○ ○ ○ ○

Absolutely no crusts to roll out! You can make magnificent ice cream pies using store-bought or homemade cookie crumb crusts. If you buy the crust, you can choose among graham cracker, shortbread, chocolate wafer, and Oreo cookie crusts. If you decide to make your own, you can use the same cookies or crushed sugar cones, amaretti, shortbread (yours or one from the supermarket), oatmeal cookies, gingersnaps, or lemon snaps. Or make a shredded coconut, meringue, or even a brownie crust (see the recipes on pages 80–82).

An ice cream pie made in a 9-inch pie pan, which holds 2 to 3 pints of ice cream, serves 8 to 12. If you'd like, make a tart instead of a pie, using a fluted 9-inch tart pan with a removable bottom. All of these recipes can be made in either a tart or a pie pan.

Ice cream pies can be as simple and elegant as a chocolate cookie crust filled with chocolate ice cream, drizzled with chocolate sauce, and sprinkled with toasted sliced almonds, or as elaborate as you'd like. Layer the ice cream, gelato, frozen yogurt, and/or sorbet with crushed cookies or candies, thick rich sauces, nuts, chocolate, syrups, fruit toppings, or liqueurs, or serve them topped with luscious sauces and whipped cream.

● *Tips for Making Ice Cream Pies*

- For the cookie crusts, put the cookies into a self-sealing plastic bag and crush them with a rolling pin; or pulse them in a food processor until finely ground.
- Freeze the crusts for at least 30 minutes to firm them before filling, so the crumbs will not mix with the ice cream.

- Brush any of the crusts with melted chocolate before filling for an extra dimension of pleasure.
- Slightly soften premium brands of ice cream for 20 minutes in the refrigerator, store brands for about 10 minutes.
- Don't let the ice cream melt while filling the pie, or it may become icy when it freezes again. To avoid the problem, just pop the ice cream back into the freezer for a few minutes, then proceed.
- If you want a distinct striped look, freeze each layer before adding the next. Or if you want a ripple or more relaxed effect, swirl each layer around a little.
- Sprinkle crushed candies, cookies, or meringues between the layers of ice cream to add textural interest. Good preserves are also wonderful. If you simply drizzle liqueur between layers, it will not freeze, because of the alcohol content; instead, swirl it into the ice cream layer before freezing, so you won't have seeping liquid between the layers.
- For storing, cover the top of ice cream pies with wax paper. Plastic wrap can tear when cold, and the dessert might dry out or absorb other flavors. And wax paper won't scrunch up and dig into the pie. Then cover the pie with a sheet of aluminum foil. Or, if you're using a store-bought crust, simply save the lid and use it when storing the pie.
- Allow ice cream pies to soften for up to 20 minutes in the refrigerator or 5 to 10 minutes at room temperature before serving.
- Use the same cookie crumbs used for the crusts as a garnish for the pies.
- Hold a warm, damp towel against the bottom of the pie plate or tart pan for a minute or two, to make it easier to serve. Then dip the knife in a glass of hot water and dry it with a towel between cuts.

ice cream pie

In one of my earliest restaurant jobs, I made at least ten of these first thing every morning, using coffee ice cream. Even without intensive practice, you'll find ice cream pies as impressive as they are delicious.

serves 8

One 9-inch Cookie Crumb Pie or Tart Crust
(page 79), made with chocolate wafers, or
store-bought chocolate wafer crust, baked
according to package directions
2 pints vanilla ice cream, slightly softened
Cool Chocolate Sauce (page 175), Lighter
Chocolate Sauce (page 176), Chocolate
Raspberry Sauce (page 177), or store-bought
chocolate sauce
Toasted sliced almonds for garnish

1.   Freeze the crust for 30 minutes.
2.   Scoop the ice cream into the crust and spread it evenly with a rubber spatula, mounding it slightly in the center. Cover the pie with wax paper and then with aluminum foil. Freeze for at least 4 hours, or up to 2 weeks.

3.   To serve, drizzle some of the chocolate sauce over the pie and sprinkle with the almonds. Let sit at room temperature for 5 to 10 minutes or in the refrigerator for up to 20 minutes, then cut into wedges. Pass additional sauce at the table.

THree-Layer sorBeT Pie

Transfer the pie from the pan to a serving plate or cake stand, if you'd like. This is also exquisite made with fruit ice creams and served with a fruit topping or sauce, or try cinnamon, pumpkin, and vanilla ice cream, with a gingersnap crust.

serves 8

One 9-inch Cookie Crumb Pie or Tart Crust (page 79), made with sugar cones, or store-bought shortbread crust, baked according to package directions
1 pint raspberry sorbet, slightly softened
1 pint lime sorbet, slightly softened
1 pint mango sorbet, slightly softened
Slightly Sweetened Whipped Cream (page 209)
Finely chopped mangoes tossed with fresh raspberries and fresh lime juice, optional

1. Freeze the crust for 30 minutes.

2. Scoop the raspberry sorbet into the crust and spread it evenly with a rubber spatula. Freeze for at least 30 minutes, or until firm.

3. Scoop the lime sorbet into the crust and spread it evenly with a rubber spatula. Freeze for at least 30 minutes, or until firm.

4. Scoop the mango sorbet into the crust and spread it evenly with a rubber spatula. Cover the pie with wax paper and then with aluminum foil. Freeze for at least 5 hours, or up to 2 weeks.

5. About 20 minutes before serving, spread the whipped cream over the pie, leaving a 1-inch band of sorbet showing around the edge. Top with the fruit, if using, and serve or refrigerate for up to 15 minutes. Cut into wedges to serve.

marbleized ice cream pie

The flavor possibilities for this pie are endless. Use any ice creams and/or sorbets that strongly contrast with each other and whose flavors harmonize.

serves 8

One 9-inch Cookie Crumb Pie or Tart Crust
     (page 79), made with chocolate wafers, or
     store-bought chocolate wafer crust, baked
     according to package directions
1 pint vanilla ice cream, slightly softened
1 pint chocolate ice cream, slightly softened
Warm Chocolate Sauce (page 175),
     Serious Chocolate Sauce (page 176),
     or store-bought chocolate sauce
Slightly Sweetened Whipped Cream (page 209)
     or one of the variations

1. Freeze the crust for 30 minutes.

2. Drop alternate scoops of both of the ice creams into the crust. Swirl them together with the tip of a small knife to marbleize them. Cover the pie with wax paper and then with aluminum foil. Freeze for at least 4 hours, or up to 2 weeks.

3. To serve, drizzle some of the chocolate sauce over the pie and let sit at room temperature for 5 to 10 minutes. Cut the pie into wedges and serve with the whipped cream, passing additional sauce at the table.

s'mores ice cream pie

This pie should only be made with a graham cracker crust, or it won't be a s'mores pie.

serves 8

One 9-inch Cookie Crumb Pie or Tart Crust
(page 79), made with graham crackers, or
store-bought graham cracker crust, baked
according to package directions
1 cup marshmallow cream
Cool Chocolate Sauce (page 175) or store-bought
chocolate sauce
2 pints chocolate and/or vanilla ice cream, slightly
softened
Miniature chocolate chips or chocolate curls
(see page xxxviii), optional

1. Freeze the crust for 30 minutes.

2. Spread the marshmallow cream in the bottom
of the crust and drizzle with ⅓ cup of the chocolate
sauce. Scoop 1 pint of the ice cream into the crust
and spread it evenly with a rubber spatula. Drizzle
with another ⅓ cup chocolate sauce. Scoop the
remaining 1 pint of ice cream into the crust and
spread it evenly, mounding it slightly in the center.
Cover the pie with wax paper and then with aluminum foil. Freeze for at least 4 hours, or up to
2 weeks.

3. To serve, sprinkle the pie with the chocolate
chips, if using, and let sit at room temperature for
5 to 10 minutes. Cut into wedges, and pass additional sauce at the table.

HOT FUDGE SUNDAE TART

This recipe is a blueprint for pleasure and for many fabulous desserts. Use strawberry instead of vanilla ice cream, or spread a layer of sugared strawberries over the vanilla ice cream. Or scoop one or several different sorbet flavors on top instead of the chocolate ice cream. For best results, use a dipper that holds ¼ to ⅓ cup for the scoops of ice cream. Use any type of crust you like.

serves 8

One 9-inch Cookie Crumb Pie or Tart Crust (page 79), made with chocolate wafers, or store-bought chocolate wafer pie crust, baked according to package directions
1 pint vanilla ice cream, slightly softened
1 to 2 pints chocolate ice cream, slightly softened
Easiest Hot Fudge Sauce (page 173), Old-fashioned Hot Fudge Sauce (page 174), or store-bought fudge sauce

1. Freeze the crust for 30 minutes.
2. Scoop the vanilla ice cream into the crust and spread it evenly with a rubber spatula.
3. Scoop round balls of the chocolate ice cream and arrange them on the vanilla ice cream. Loosely cover the pie with wax paper and then with aluminum foil. Freeze for at least 4 hours, or up to 2 weeks.
4. To serve, let the pie sit at room temperature for 5 to 10 minutes. Drizzle with some of the hot fudge sauce, cut into wedges, and pass additional sauce at the table.

cookie crumb pie or tart crust

You can use crushed sugar cones or your favorite cookies to make this crust. I suggest:

Chocolate wafers

Graham crackers and chocolate graham crackers

Shortbread

Gingersnaps

Oatmeal cookies

Amaretti

Peanut butter cookies

Sandwich cookies

Coconut cookies

MAKES ONE 9-INCH PIE SHELL

FOR A 9-INCH GLASS PIE PLATE

1½ cups cookie crumbs

5 tablespoon unsalted butter, melted

FOR A 9-INCH FLUTED TART PAN WITH A REMOVABLE BOTTOM

2 cups cookie crumbs

6 tablespoons unsalted butter, melted

1. Position a rack in the middle of the oven and preheat the oven to 350 degrees F. Butter the pie plate or tart pan.

2. To make the cookie crumbs, either pulse the cookies in a food processor or place the cookies in a heavy-duty self-sealing plastic bag and crush them with a rolling pin.

3. Stir the crumbs and butter together in a bowl until the crumbs are evenly moistened. Transfer to the pie plate or tart pan, and, using your fingers, press the mixture evenly into the bottom and up the sides of the pan.

4. Bake for 8 to 10 minutes, until toasted. Cool completely on a wire rack.

chocolate lovers
take note

Any of these crusts can be spread with 2 ounces melted bittersweet, semisweet, milk, or white chocolate before chilling.

COCONUT PIE SHELL

Fill this with all things tropical! Try coconut gelato and/or coconut sorbet, or mango, passion fruit, pineapple, banana, guava, lemongrass, lime, or piña colada sorbet or ice cream. Don't forget that chocolate is tropical too—a tiny drizzle of sauce over the finished pie would be a treat.

MAKES ONE 9-INCH PIE SHELL

2 cups (6 ounces) sweetened shredded coconut
Toasted coconut for garnish, optional

1. Position a rack in the center of the oven and preheat the oven to 325 degrees F. Generously butter a 9-inch glass pie plate.

2. Put the coconut in a medium bowl and break up any clumps with your fingertips. Press the coconut evenly over the bottom and up the sides of the pie plate.

3. Bake for 12 to 15 minutes, until the edges of the crust are golden brown. Cool completely on a wire rack. After filling with ice cream, garnish with toasted coconut, if using.

meringue pie shell

In spring and summer, fill this with scoops of vanilla and/or fruit-flavored ice cream and/or raspberry or other berry or fruit sorbet, and top with mixed ripe berries or sliced fruits. In the cold season, go the caramel route, using caramel ice cream, caramel sauce, and toasted pine nuts. For chocolate lovers, use chocolate ice cream and one of the many chocolate or hot fudge sauces in this book.

MAKES ONE 9-INCH PIE SHELL

3 large egg whites
¼ teaspoon salt
½ cup sugar

1. Position a rack in the middle of the oven and preheat the oven to 325 degrees F.

2. In a large bowl, beat the egg whites with an electric mixer on medium-high speed until foamy. Add the salt and beat until the egg whites just form soft peaks when the beaters are lifted. Add the sugar 1 tablespoon at a time, beating well after each addition, and continue beating just until the egg whites form stiff peaks when the beaters are lifted.

3. Spread the meringue evenly over the bottom and up the sides of a 9-inch glass pie plate. Bake for about 20 minutes, or until dry but not browned. Cool completely on a wire rack.

Brownie Pie Shell

This pie shell is perfect for chocolate lovers.

MAKES ONE 9-INCH PIE SHELL

½ cup packed light brown sugar

3 ounces bittersweet or semisweet chocolate,
    finely chopped

3 tablespoons unsalted butter

½ cup all-purpose flour

¼ teaspoon baking powder

Pinch of salt

1 large egg, at room temperature

1 teaspoon pure vanilla extract

1. Position a rack in the middle of the oven and preheat the oven to 325 degrees F. Generously butter a 9-inch glass pie plate.

2. Melt the sugar, chocolate, and butter with 2 tablespoons water in a medium heatproof bowl set over a saucepan of simmering water, whisking until smooth. Remove the bowl and let the chocolate cool to room temperature.

3. Whisk together the flour, baking powder, and salt in a medium bowl.

4. Whisk the egg and vanilla into the chocolate mixture. Whisk in the flour mixture just until blended.

5. Spread the batter evenly in the pie plate. Bake for 20 to 25 minutes, until a cake tester inserted in the center comes out clean. Cool completely on a wire rack. With a small metal spatula carefully loosen the brownie from the pie plate (but do not remove).

Chocolate wafer crust with raspberry sorbet and chocolate ice cream or sorbet and
Chocolate Raspberry Sauce (page 177)

Chocolate wafer crust with coffee ice cream, topped with warm Old-fashioned Caramel
Sauce (page 181)

Chocolate wafer crust with mint chip ice cream, drizzled with crème de menthe and
garnished with chopped chocolate-covered mints

Chocolate wafer crust with cherry ice cream and Cherry Sauce (page 191) or chocolate
sauce; or with rocky road ice cream and Easiest Marshmallow Sauce (page 185)

Graham cracker crust with peach ice cream, topped with Peach Whipped Cream (page
209) and served with sliced ripe peaches

Graham cracker crust with banana ice cream, topped with Old-fashioned Caramel Sauce
(page 181)

Graham cracker crust with dulce de leche ice cream, topped with fine graham cracker
crumbs

Gingersnap crust with chocolate gelato, topped with chocolate curls (see page xxxviii) and
finely ground gingersnaps

Gingersnap crust with blueberry ice cream, topped with whipped cream and Blueberry
Sauce (page 185)

Shortbread crust with strawberry ice cream, served with Sliced Strawberry Topping (page
188), or Strawberries and Basil (page 147), and Strawberry Whipped Cream (page 209)

Shortbread crust with chocolate ice cream and bananas thinly sliced on the diagonal,
drizzled with chocolate sauce

Oatmeal cookie crust with butterscotch ice cream, garnished with crushed Praline
(page xxxix)

Sugar cone crust with peach ice cream and Old-fashioned Caramel Sauce (page 181)

Coconut crust with coconut gelato and mango sorbet, topped with Blackberry Sauce
(page 187)

Ice cream cakes are crowd-pleasers, and they're a great way to put all your favorites into one festive dessert. They're also very easy to make—just soften the ice cream a bit and layer it in a pan.

● *Tips for Making Ice Cream Cakes*

If the ice cream begins to melt at any time while you're assembling the cake, refreeze it before continuing. If it thaws completely it may be icy when it's refrozen, although the fat in super-premium ice cream will be protection against ice crystals forming.

To spread the ice cream, scoop it into the pan and quickly spread it with a flexible rubber spatula or small offset metal spatula, dipped in warm water as needed.

If you want to serve only part of an ice cream cake, don't garnish it until you're ready to serve, and store the remainder wrapped very well.

SKY-HIGH Layered ice cream cake

This is a tremendously versatile recipe. You might use sorbet, other flavors of ice cream, and/or gelato. Try any thick sauce, such as chocolate, caramel, marshmallow, fruit, or berry, and garnish with crushed candies, cookies, or other nuts.

serves 12

3 pints chocolate gelato or ice cream, slightly softened

One 13-ounce jar Nutella or other chocolate hazelnut spread

2 pints hazelnut gelato or ice cream, slightly softened

1 cup coarsely chopped toasted hazelnuts

1. Spoon the chocolate gelato in small pieces into a 9-inch springform pan, filling in any large holes, then spread it evenly with a warm rubber spatula. Pour half of the Nutella over the gelato and spread it evenly with a small offset spatula. Freeze for at least 1 hour, or until firm.

2. Spoon the hazelnut gelato over the Nutella in small pieces, filling in any large holes, then spread it evenly with a warm rubber spatula. Pour the remaining Nutella over the gelato and spread it evenly with the offset spatula. Scatter the hazelnuts over the top of the cake, then press in. Cover the pan tightly with aluminum foil and freeze for at least 6 hours, or up to 2 weeks.

3. To serve, let the cake stand at room temperature for 5 to 10 minutes or in the refrigerator for 15 to 20 minutes. Run a knife around the inside of the pan, release the side of the pan, and remove it. Cut the cake into wedges.

meringue ice cream (or sorbet) cake

Sometimes the ideal party dessert is one that can be made in advance—then you have one less thing to worry about. Here's one that can be made up to two weeks ahead.

serves 12

1½ cups sugar

2 tablespoons cornstarch

6 large egg whites

¼ teaspoon salt

1½ teaspoons pure vanilla extract

2 pints vanilla ice cream, slightly softened

¾ cup Cool Chocolate Sauce (page 175) or
　　store-bought chocolate sauce

1. Position the oven racks in the top and bottom third of the oven and preheat the oven to 300 degrees F. Trace two 8-inch circles on each of two sheets of parchment paper. Place each piece of paper on a large baking sheet.

2. Whisk ½ cup of the sugar and the cornstarch together in a small bowl.

3. In a large deep bowl, beat the egg whites with an electric mixer on medium speed until foamy. Increase the speed to medium-high, add the salt, and beat just until the egg whites form soft peaks when the beaters are lifted. Add the remaining 1 cup sugar 1 tablespoon at a time, beating well after each addition, and continue beating just until the egg whites form stiff peaks when the beaters are lifted. With a whisk or a rubber spatula, fold in the reserved sugar mixture and the vanilla.

4. Spoon the meringue onto the paper circles, using about 2 cups for each circle, and smooth it with a rubber spatula. Bake the meringues, switching the position of the sheets after 30 minutes, for 1 hour, or until light golden brown. Let cool on the sheets on wire racks.

5. Peel off the parchment paper from the meringues. Set aside the least attractive meringue to use for the garnish. Fit 1 meringue into a 10-inch springform pan. Spread about 1⅓ cups of the ice cream and then about ¼ cup of the sauce over it. Top with another meringue and spread with another 1⅓ cups ice cream and ¼ cup sauce. Add 1 more meringue and top with the remaining ice cream and sauce. Crumble the reserved meringue and sprinkle it over the top. Cover the pan tightly with aluminum foil and freeze for at least 6 hours, or up to 2 weeks.

6. To serve, let the cake stand at room temperature for 5 to 10 minutes or in the refrigerator for 15 to 20 minutes. Run a table knife around the inside of the pan, release the side of the pan, and remove it. Cut the cake into wedges.

Ice cream, frozen yogurt, and gelato: Instead of vanilla, try black walnut, coffee, or green tea; or butter pecan or dulce de leche, with Scottish-Style Butterscotch Sauce (page 183); chocolate, with Easiest Marshmallow Sauce (page 185); cherry, with Cherry Sauce (page 191) or chocolate sauce; blueberry, with Blueberry Sauce (page 185); peach, with Raspberry Plum Sauce (page 190); rose petal, with Smooth Strawberry Sauce (page 188); tiramisù, with chocolate or Coffee Sauce (page 184); milk chocolate, with Milk Chocolate–Peanut Butter Sauce (page 179), or eggnog, with Hot Buttered Rum Sauce (page 184).

Sorbet: Along with vanilla ice cream (use 1 pint each ice cream and sorbet), try blackberry, Meyer lemon, raspberry, strawberry, chocolate, coconut, tangerine, blueberry, cassis, ginger-lemon, margarita, tropical, peach, rainbow, pineapple, green apple, or passion fruit sorbet. Mix and match with different fruit sauces.

pound cake ice cream cake

Feel free to use any flavor ice cream, frozen yogurt, or sorbet; use two or three flavors, and layer them in the cake. You can also drizzle the cake with a tiny bit of chocolate sauce before serving and serve it with Sliced Strawberry Topping (page 188), or the sauce of your choice.

serves 12

Nine 3 × 2 × ½-inch thick slices pound cake
3 pints strawberry ice cream, slightly softened
Slightly Sweetened Whipped Cream (page 209)
　　or Strawberry Whipped Cream (page 209)

1. Arrange the cake slices in a single layer in the bottom of a 9-inch springform pan, cutting them to fit as necessary. Freeze for at least 30 minutes.

2. Spoon the ice cream over the cake in small pieces, filling in any large holes, then spread it evenly with a warm rubber spatula. Cover the pan tightly with aluminum foil. Freeze for at least 6 hours, or up to 2 weeks.

3. To serve, let the cake stand at room temperature for 5 to 10 minutes or in the refrigerator for 15 to 20 minutes. Run a table knife around the inside of the pan, release the side of the pan, and remove it. Spread the whipped cream evenly over the top of the cake, and cut into wedges.

cookie crumb ice cream cake

I especially love this with gingersnap crumbs and strawberry ice cream. You can also substitute about ¾ cup crushed amaretti and ¼ cup ground hazelnuts for the cookie crumbs.

serves 12

1½ cups chocolate wafer cookie crumbs
2 pints chocolate ice cream, slightly softened
1 pint vanilla ice cream, slightly softened
1 pint coffee ice cream, slightly softened
Slightly Sweetened Whipped Cream (page 209),
    Chocolate Whipped Cream (page 210),
    or Coffee Whipped Cream (page 210)

1. Generously butter the bottom and sides of a 9-inch springform pan. Sprinkle the bottom evenly with ½ cup of the cookie crumbs. Freeze for at least 30 minutes.

2. Spoon the chocolate ice cream in small pieces over the crumbs, filling in any large holes, then spread it evenly with a warm rubber spatula. Sprinkle evenly with ⅓ cup of the cookie crumbs. Freeze for at least 30 minutes, or until firm.

3. Spoon the vanilla ice cream in small pieces over the crumbs, filling in any large holes, then spread it evenly with a warm rubber spatula. Sprinkle evenly

with another ⅓ cup of the cookie crumbs. Cover tightly and freeze for at least 30 minutes, or until firm.

4. Spoon the coffee ice cream in small pieces over the crumbs, filling in any large holes, then spread it evenly with a warm rubber spatula. Sprinkle evenly with the remaining ⅓ cup of the cookie crumbs. Cover the pan tightly with aluminum foil. Freeze for at least 6 hours, or up to 2 weeks.

5. To serve, let the cake stand at room temperature for 5 to 10 minutes or in the refrigerator for 15 to 20 minutes. Run a table knife around the inside of the pan, release the side of the pan, and remove it. Spread the whipped cream evenly over the top of the cake, and cut into wedges.

CHOCOLATE TRUFFLE ICE CREAM LAYER CAKE

This recipe is adapted from Dorie Greenspan's Sweet Times, *one of my all-time favorite books. She adds raspberries to the ice cream. You can use any ice cream, gelato, or sorbet flavors you choose. Be careful when you spread the ice cream over the chocolate mixture, as it doesn't freeze solid.*

serves 12

9 ounces bittersweet or semisweet chocolate,
    finely chopped

14 tablespoons (1¾ sticks) unsalted butter,
    cut into small pieces

½ cup granulated sugar

8 large eggs, at room temperature

2 pints vanilla ice cream, slightly softened

2 pints cherry or raspberry sorbet, slightly
    softened

Chocolate shavings (see page xxxviii), optional

Cherries on the stem or fresh raspberries, optional

Confectioners' sugar for dusting, optional

1. Generously butter the bottom and sides of a 9-inch springform pan.

2. Combine the chocolate, butter, and sugar in a heatproof bowl, set it over a saucepan of simmering water, and whisk until the chocolate is melted and smooth. Remove the bowl from the heat and let stand for 5 minutes.

3. Whisk the eggs one at a time into the chocolate mixture, then whisk until well blended. Pour 1½ cups of the chocolate mixture into the prepared pan. Freeze for at least 30 minutes, until firm. Cover the remaining chocolate mixture and set aside at room temperature.

4. Spoon the ice cream in small pieces over the chocolate, filling in any large holes, then spread it evenly with a warm rubber spatula. Pour half of the remaining chocolate mixture over the frozen ice cream layer. Freeze for at least 30 minutes, until firm.

5. Spoon the sorbet in small pieces over the chocolate, filling in any large holes, then spread it evenly with a warm rubber spatula. Pour the remaining chocolate mixture over the sorbet. Cover the pan tightly with aluminum foil. Freeze for at least 6 hours, or up to 2 weeks.

6. To serve, let the cake stand at room temperature for 5 to 10 minutes or in the refrigerator for 15 to 20 minutes. Run a table knife around the inside of the pan, release the side of the pan, and remove it. Garnish the top of the cake with chocolate shavings and/or cherries, and a light sifting of confectioners' sugar, if using, and cut into wedges.

Ice cream and meringue make one of the best combinations of textures in the culinary world. Whether it's the soft meringue on a Baked Alaska or a crunchy, melt-in-your-mouth, firmer meringue shell, it's always been one of my favorite ways to enjoy ice cream and sorbet. You can buy meringue shells at pastry shops in a wide variety of flavors, colors, and sizes. Fill the shells, large or small, with scoops of ice cream, in any size, and freeze until serving time.

You can also add flavorings to the meringues you make yourself. Try finely grated citrus zest, chocolate sprinkles, unsweetened cocoa powder, miniature chocolate chips, toasted nuts, chocolate nibs, flavoring extracts, minced crystallized ginger, finely ground pistachios, or rose water. A cocoa powder meringue filled with chocolate sorbet and/or ice cream and sprinkled with cocoa powder makes an unusual and very finished-looking dessert. You might even add Chocolate Whipped Cream (page 210). Or try hazelnut meringues with chocolate and coffee ice cream, walnut meringues with butter brickle ice cream, or almond meringues with peach and/or strawberry ice cream.

I prefer crunchy meringues to hard ones. I like their texture better—a little chewy in the middle—and because they get a little brown, I think they have better flavor. You can make meringue shells up to three days ahead of serving and store them in an airtight container or tightly wrapped.

The combination of frozen desserts and meringue takes well to seasonal ripe fruits and berries and sauces. Try peach Melba ice cream in meringue shells with sliced ripe peaches and Raspberry Sauce (page 187), or chocolate ice cream and cherry, peach, or strawberry sauce. Then top with whipped cream.

easiest baked alaska

Buy the pound cake and the ice cream, then all you need to do is beat some egg whites. Originally created in Europe and called Crème Norvégienne, Baked Alaska was made popular at Delmonico's restaurant in New York City in the late nineteenth century. The dessert always makes a dramatic entrance, and this is the easiest one ever. The flavor possibilities are endless—you'll probably have to make at least a few. This recipe is for large slices of pound cake; if your loaves are small (like frozen Sara Lee pound cake, only 2 inches high by 3¼ inches wide), use 2 slices per serving, and place them bottom to bottom on the baking sheet.

serves 4

Four ¾-inch-thick slices homemade or
    store-bought pound cake
¼ cup orange or other liqueur
2 pints vanilla ice cream
4 large egg whites, at room temperature
½ cup sugar
½ teaspoon pure vanilla extract

1. Arrange the cake slices several inches apart on a baking sheet. Brush each slice with 1 tablespoon of the liqueur. Top the slices with scoops of the ice cream. Freeze, tightly covered, for at least 20 minutes, or up to 8 hours.

2. Position a rack in the middle of the oven and preheat the oven to 475 degrees F.

3. In a large bowl, beat the egg whites with an electric mixer on medium-high speed until they form soft peaks when the beaters are lifted. Add the sugar 1 tablespoon at a time, then beat until the egg whites form stiff peaks when the beaters are lifted. Beat in the vanilla.

4. Immediately spread the meringue over the ice cream and cake, using a rubber spatula to create a smooth domed top for each one and making certain that the meringue touches the cake all around the edges to seal in the ice cream. If desired, form swirls in the meringue using a small spoon, starting at the center top of each mound. Immediately place in the oven and bake for 4 to 5 minutes, until the meringue is lightly browned.

5. Using a wide spatula, transfer each Baked Alaska to a serving plate and serve immediately.

Ice cream, frozen yogurt, and gelato: Instead of vanilla, try chocolate, coffee, coconut, hazelnut, tiramisù, lemon, peanut butter fudge, peach, caramel, ginger, cinnamon, orange, cookies and cream, almond praline, peppermint, triple caramel chunk, turtle sundae, cherry vanilla, pistachio, or white chocolate ice cream. Or use half vanilla ice cream and half sorbet: raspberry, mango, passion fruit, cassis, strawberry, or lemon.

Not necessary, but dazzling and divine: Serve the Baked Alaskas in a pool of fruit or berry sauce or with a fruit topping on the side. Or serve sprinkled with miniature chocolate chips, chopped toasted hazelnuts, or crushed peppermint candies.

*Ice cream is eaten with a spoon,
but when served as part of Baked Alaska or with cake,
it is eaten with a dessert fork and spoon.*

✻

—NANCY DUNNAN AND NANCY TUCKERMAN, *THE AMY VANDERBILT
COMPLETE BOOK OF ETIQUETTE, ENTIRELY REWRITTEN AND UPDATED*

pavlova

Pavlova is one of the national dishes of Australia, and with good reason—it's a scrumptious treat. There the meringue shell is more likely to be filled with whipped cream than ice cream, but it is very lovely with ice cream and fruit. Don't use wax paper, as the meringue will stick. Parchment paper is available in most supermarkets.

serves 8

FOR THE MERINGUE

4 large egg whites, at room temperature
¼ teaspoon cream of tartar
Pinch of salt
1 cup granulated sugar

1 to 2 pints vanilla or strawberry ice cream
1 cup mixed fresh berries
Confectioners' sugar for dusting

1. Position a rack in the middle of the oven and preheat the oven to 225 degrees F. Trace a 9-inch circle on a sheet of parchment paper. Place the paper on a baking sheet.

2. In a large bowl, beat the egg whites with an electric mixer on medium speed until foamy. Increase the speed to medium-high, add the cream of tartar and salt, and beat just until the egg whites form soft peaks when the beaters are lifted. Add the granulated sugar 1 tablespoon at a time, then continue to beat just until the whites form stiff peaks when the beaters are lifted.

3. Spoon the meringue onto the 9-inch circle, scooping the sides upward to form a nest. (Or spoon the meringue into a pastry bag fitted with a large star tip. Starting at the outside edge, pipe a spiral of meringue to fill the circle. Holding the pastry bag upright, pipe a ring of rosettes along the edge for the rim, then pipe a second tier of rosettes on the shoulders of the first ring.) Bake for 1 hour, or until the meringue is dry to the touch. Turn off the oven and leave the meringue in the oven for 2 hours.

4. Meanwhile, place a baking sheet lined with wax paper in the freezer for 10 minutes. Scoop the ice cream into large or small balls and place on the baking sheet. Freeze, covered, for at least 30 minutes, or up to 1 day.

5. Peel the paper off the meringue. Store, tightly wrapped, at room temperature until ready to use.

6. Just before serving, place the ice cream scoops in the meringue shell. Arrange the berries on top, and lightly sift confectioners' sugar over the berries. Cut into wedges and serve immediately.

INDIVIDUAL meringue nests

These are good filled with any berry or other fruit ice cream and sauce, or with caramel ice cream and caramel sauce.

serves 8

4 large egg whites, at room temperature
¼ teaspoon cream of tartar
Pinch of salt
½ cup sugar
2 pints chocolate ice cream
Serious Chocolate Sauce (page 176) or
    store-bought chocolate sauce, warmed

1. Position the oven racks in the top and bottom third of the oven and preheat the oven to 225 degrees F. Trace four 4-inch circles on each of two sheets of parchment paper. Place the paper on two large baking sheets.

2. In a large bowl, beat the egg whites with an electric mixer on medium speed until foamy. Add the cream of tartar and salt, increase the speed to medium-high, and beat just until the egg whites form soft peaks when the beaters are lifted. Add the sugar 1 tablespoon at a time, and continue to beat just until the whites form stiff peaks when the beaters are lifted.

3. Spoon the meringue onto the 4-inch circles, using a scant ½ cup meringue for each one and scooping the sides upward to form nests. Bake, switching the position of the sheets halfway through, for 1 hour, or until the meringues are dry to the touch. Turn off the oven and leave the meringues in the oven for 2 hours.

4. Meanwhile, place a large plate or a baking sheet lined with wax paper in the freezer for 10 minutes. Scoop the ice cream into 8 large balls and place on the baking sheet. Freeze, covered, for at least 30 minutes, or up to 1 day.

5. Peel the paper off the meringues. Store, tightly wrapped, at room temperature until ready to use.

6. Just before serving, place the ice cream in the meringue shells. Drizzle with the chocolate sauce, and serve immediately.

all-american eton mess

This is always served on Prize Day at Eton school in England. There Eton Mess is broken-up meringues, sliced strawberries, and heavy cream. I think it's much better with ice cream—probably another instance where the English can't believe how much and how often we Americans miss the point. But I bet you'll be on my side.

serves 8

Meringue from Pavlova (page 94)
2 pints vanilla ice cream
Sliced Strawberry Topping (page 188)

Crumble the meringue into eight serving bowls. Top with the ice cream and then the strawberries. Serve immediately.

the ice cream lover's pantry

If you have ice cream in the freezer, you have dessert. But for an extraordinary, still easy dessert, keep the following ingredients on hand in your pantry to toss together with ice cream for quick and stunning treats.

cookies

Crushed, these can be used as a topping, in layered desserts, for quick pie crusts, and to make Ice Cream Truffles (page 102).

nuts

These are indispensable for topping sundaes, coating balls of ice cream, and dipping cones in.

candies

A sprinkle of candies from crushed English toffee to gummy worms can make any ice cream dessert more fun.

liqueurs and spirits

If you're serving adults, simply topping ice cream with a splash of liqueur turns it into a special treat. You can also use liqueurs and spirits to flavor homemade or store-bought sauces, syrups, and whipped cream.

preserves

Layer fruit preserves in ice cream cakes and pies, placing a spoonful into meringues before adding the ice cream or sorbet; use for super-quick "In a Jam" Sauce (page 194); or stir into other sauces, syrups, and whipped creams.

syrups

Use store-bought (or homemade) syrups for sundaes, coupes, splits, parfaits, and fountain drinks; layer in ice cream cakes and pies; drizzle over any frozen dessert.

sauces

Sauces make an ice cream dessert a special occasion. Make your own from the sauce chapter (page 169) or see page 196 for ideas for using store-bought sauces.

sodas

Keep root beer and other sodas on hand for almost instant ice cream floats.

FROZEN ASSETS: SNOWBALLS, TRUFFLES, TERRINES, AND BOMBES

● ● ● ● ○ ○ ○ ○

tartufos

Tartufo means "truffle" in Italian, but these only look like truffles. They're chocolate-coated gelato balls with a treat buried in the center. They don't have to be perfectly round spheres; in fact, they shouldn't be.

serves 4

1 pint vanilla gelato or ice cream, slightly softened
4 toasted whole hazelnuts, plus ¼ cup finely
　　chopped toasted hazelnuts
2 ounces bittersweet or semisweet chocolate,
　　finely chopped
Slightly Sweetened Whipped Cream (page 209)
　　or Chocolate Whipped Cream (page 210)

1. Place a plate lined with wax paper in the freezer for 10 minutes.

2. Working quickly, with a large scoop, scoop a ball of the gelato, using ½ cup. With the gelato still in the scoop, gently press a whole hazelnut into the center of the ball, then reshape the ball around the hazelnut. Place the ball on the wax-paper-lined plate and repeat to make three more balls. Freeze for 30 minutes, or until firm.

3. Stir together the chopped hazelnuts and chocolate on a plate. Roll the gelato balls in the mixture to coat completely, return them to the wax-paper-lined plate, cover, and freeze for at least 1 hour, or up to 2 days.

4. To serve, mound the whipped cream in the centers of four chilled plates. Top with the tartufos, and serve immediately.

snowballs

These treats resemble snowballs because of their coconut coating. If you'd like, though, you can coat them in other things—try crushed macaroons or other cookies, finely chopped toasted nuts, or crushed brittle, crushed Praline (page xxxix), or other candy. One of my favorites is peach ice cream rolled in toasted sliced almonds and served with peach, raspberry, or chocolate sauce. For toasting coconut, see page 207.

serves 4

1 pint vanilla ice cream, slightly softened
1 cup toasted sweetened shredded coconut
Warm Chocolate Sauce (page 175), Serious
    Chocolate Sauce (page 176), or store-bought
    chocolate sauce, warmed

1. Place a plate lined with wax paper in the freezer for 10 minutes.
2. Working quickly, with a large scoop, scoop 4 balls of the ice cream, using ½ cup for each snowball. Place the balls on the wax-paper-lined plate and freeze for 30 minutes, or until firm.
3. Place the toasted coconut on a sheet of wax paper. Roll the ice cream balls in the coconut to coat completely, return to the wax-paper-lined plate, cover, and freeze for at least 1 hour, or up to 2 days.
4. To serve, pour about 2 tablespoons of the chocolate sauce into the center of each of four serving plates. Top with the snowballs, and serve immediately, passing additional sauce at the table.

ice cream truffles

I use Nabisco Famous Wafers in this recipe. If you don't use all of the ground wafers (you will probably have a bit left over), save them for sprinkling or layering in other ice cream desserts. You might add instant espresso powder to the crumbs, or some chopped toasted nuts, candies, or other cookies. Try pistachio–white chocolate ice cream rolled in ground chocolate wafers and finely chopped pistachios. Or use chocolate, coffee, cherry, raspberry, or hazelnut ice cream instead of the vanilla.

MAKES 28 TO 32 TRUFFLES

1 pint vanilla ice cream
18 chocolate wafers

1. Place a plate lined with wax paper in the freezer for 10 minutes.

2. With a small ice cream scoop or a melon baller, quickly scoop small balls of the ice cream, using about 1 tablespoon for each; make 3 or 4 at a time, placing them on a plate, then transferring them to the plate in the freezer. Freeze for at least 30 minutes, or until firm.

3. Pulse the wafers in a food processor until finely ground. Transfer to a sheet of wax paper.

4. Working quickly, roll the ice cream balls in the ground wafers to coat completely. Return to the wax-paper-lined plate, cover with plastic wrap, and freeze for at least 30 minutes, or up to 2 days.

5. Serve in foil bonbon cups, if desired, or simply arranged on small plates.

LEMON-SORBET-FILLED LEMONS

This is adapted from my book Luscious Lemon Desserts. *Use it as a guide for filling oranges and limes. You can use any sorbet or fruit ice cream. The hollowed-out lemons can be kept in the freezer for up to 3 days before being filled with the sorbet, but once you've filled them, they should be served within 12 hours.*

Select thick-skinned lemons—and if you can find lemons with their leaves still attached, grab them.

serves 4

4 medium lemons
1 pint lemon sorbet, slightly softened

1. Cut a lid from the top of each lemon, removing about one-quarter of the fruit, and reserve the lids. Remove a thin slice from the base of each one so the lemons will sit upright; do not cut into the pulp. With a grapefruit-sectioning knife, remove as much of the pulp from each lemon as possible, leaving the rinds intact. Reserve the pulp and juice for another use. Freeze the lemon cups and their lids, for at least 3 hours and up to 3 days.

2. Spoon the sorbet into the frozen lemon cups, mounding the tops generously. Add the lids, and freeze for at least 3 hours, or up to 12 hours.

3. To serve, place on chilled serving plates.

ice cream terrine

This couldn't be simpler. Just choose flavors that go well together, with an eye to contrasting colors and harmonious flavors. See the "Flavor Inspirations" opposite for ideas. You might also make a terrine using two different sorbets with a layer of vanilla ice cream in the middle. You can let each layer freeze before adding the next, but it isn't necessary.

serves 8

1 pint chocolate ice cream or gelato, slightly softened

1 pint vanilla ice cream or gelato, slightly softened

1 pint raspberry ice cream or gelato, slightly softened

Warm Chocolate Sauce (page 175), Raspberry Sauce (page 187), any fruit or berry sauce (see pages 185–194), or store-bought sauce

1. Line a 9 × 5-inch loaf pan with plastic wrap, leaving an overhang to make unmolding easy.

2. Spread the chocolate ice cream evenly in the pan, making sure to pack it into the corners. Top with a smooth layer of the vanilla, then the raspberry. Freeze, tightly wrapped, until very firm, at least 4 hours, or up to 3 weeks.

3. To serve, remove the pan from the freezer and let stand for several minutes. Invert the pan onto a cutting board or serving platter, and lift it off. Remove the plastic wrap. Cut the terrine into thick slices, and place on chilled serving plates. Drizzle with the sauce, and serve immediately, passing additional sauce at the table.

variation

Use a mini loaf pan, 2 inches high, 3 inches wide, and 5½ inches long. Fill it with a pint of ice cream, gelato, or sorbet, or layer different flavors as above, using about ⅔ cup for each layer. Or do the expedient thing: Use three pans and three flavors, and fill the pans with a layer of each flavor. Then you can serve one terrine and have two in the freezer at the ready for any occasion. (A mini terrine serves 4.)

FLAVOR
INSPIRATIONS

Ice cream, frozen yogurt, and gelato: Instead of chocolate, vanilla, and raspberry, try ginger, mango, and coconut; chocolate, tiramisù, and coffee; mint chocolate chip, vanilla chocolate chip, and mocha chocolate chip; strawberry, raspberry, and blueberry; or amaretto, peach, and pistachio.

Sorbet: Instead of gelato, try cassis, pear, and raspberry; mango, coconut, and pineapple; peach, chocolate, and raspberry; coconut, chocolate, and passion fruit; or lemon, blood orange, and lime.

Not necessary, but dazzling and divine: Sprinkle finely chopped chocolate or crushed candies, Praline (page xxxix), or cookies, or drizzle sauces or fruit toppings, between the layers. Press chocolate truffles, toasted nuts, or amarena cherries (see page 196) into the ice cream.

POLKa-DOT SORBET Terrine

A little more free-form than the Ice Cream Terrine on page 104, with its even layers of flavors and colors, this dessert takes the relaxed approach. Add the brightly colored balls to the main flavor of sorbet haphazardly, so the slices will have a pleasing asymmetrical look: the goal is to cut into two or three of the "polka dots" in each slice. You might want to use three sorbet flavors—⅓ cup each of cherry, apricot, and peach tastes great in a base of lime or lemon sorbet. Or use ice cream or gelato.

serves 8

½ cup raspberry sorbet, slightly softened
½ cup mango sorbet, slightly softened
2½ pints lemon sorbet, slightly softened
Raspberry Sauce (page 187) or store-bought
    raspberry sauce

1. Place a plate lined with wax paper in the freezer for 10 minutes.

2. With a small ice cream scoop or a melon baller, quickly scoop small balls of the raspberry and mango sorbets, using a scant 1 tablespoon for each; make 3 or 4 balls at a time, placing them on a plate, then immediately transferring them to the plate in the freezer. Freeze for at least 30 minutes, or until firm.

3. Line a 9 × 5-inch loaf pan with plastic wrap, leaving an overhang to make unmolding easy. Spread about one-third of the lemon sorbet in the loaf pan, firmly packing it into the corners. Push about half of the sorbet balls into the lemon sorbet so they are at different levels. Add another third of the lemon sorbet and freeze for at least 30 minutes.

4. Add the remaining lemon sorbet and sorbet balls, burying the sorbet balls in the lemon sorbet; some of the balls can be on the top. Freeze, tightly wrapped, for at least 6 hours, or until firm.

5. To serve, remove the pan from the freezer and let it stand for several minutes. Invert the pan onto a cutting board or serving platter, and lift it off. Remove the plastic wrap. Cut the terrine into thick slices, and place on chilled serving plates. Drizzle with the sauce, and serve immediately, passing additional sauce at the table.

Bombes, from classic French cuisine, were originally made back in the days when ice blocks were used for refrigeration. They were then and are now dessert and astonishment all in one—a beautiful look, with a bit of mystery, and full of good promises. The major impact of a bombe is its shape and the layers of colors.

Traditionally bombes were made with ice cream and a mousse filling, but the recipes here use store-bought frozen desserts—there's no mousse making, just the fun part of putting a bombe together. It looks complicated, but it's really very easy. You just need to plan ahead, as bombes should be made at least a day in advance. Bombes made in simple molds are the easiest to make and the most dramatic to serve. The beautiful bands of color are irresistible.

A one-piece mold is the only way to go. Two-part molds are an invitation to frustration: They don't always seal well, and the possibility of leakage is high. Choose a small mold, 4 to 6 cups or so, with a simple, maybe architectural, shape. A 6-cup mold will make 6 to 8 servings, and it's not too often I use a larger one.

● *Tips for Making Bombes*

- Lightly oil a mold intended for gelatin, a tubular cake pan, a loaf pan, a metal bowl, or a steamed pudding mold and line it with plastic wrap before filling. (The plastic wrap may give the ice cream wrinkles, but you can smooth those out with a warmed small offset spatula after unmolding.)
- Most important is to chill the mold thoroughly before you begin, and to use chilled utensils for filling the mold.

- Molds that have some give, like aluminum cake pans, rather than rigid ones, make unmolding a little easier.
- Let the ice cream soften in the refrigerator for 20 minutes or so before filling the mold—it must be soft enough to fill in all the nooks and crannies of the mold. Use a rubber spatula or ice cream spade to fill the mold and a small offset spatula to smooth the layers.
- Let each layer freeze before adding the next one. Continue adding layers until the mold is filled, and freeze it until the ice cream is firm before unmolding. How long that will take depends on how large the mold is, how cold your freezer is, and other such variables, but you should figure on up to 6 hours for a 1½-quart mold, less for a smaller one.
- Pack the ice cream firmly so it takes on the pattern of the mold.
- Dusting the top of the bombe with chopped nuts or cake or cookie crumbs before unmolding it onto a serving plate will help keep the bombe from sliding around on the plate.
- To unmold the bombe, run a table knife or thin metal spatula around the edge, and cover the outside of the mold with a warm damp towel. Invert the mold onto a chilled serving dish, with the warm towel still around it. The heat will soften the surface just enough to let the bombe slip out. Return the unmolded bombe to the freezer until you are ready to serve it.
- To serve, take the bombe out of the freezer and let it stand for a few minutes at room temperature. Add any garnish, and take the bombe to the table. Use a wide pastry server or cake knife, dipping the server or knife in warm water between cuts.

Line a smooth mold or a bowl with a layer of raspberries, nuts, or blueberries.

Add layers of sauces, fresh fruit, crumbled cookies or candies, or toasted nuts for color and textural contrasts. Keep layers of cookies, candies, or nuts thin, or the layers will separate after unmolding.

three-layer ice cream bombe

Be sure to present the bombe to your dinner partners before serving, for greatest dramatic effect.

serves 6 to 8

1 pint chocolate ice cream, slightly softened
1 pint vanilla ice cream, slightly softened
1 pint coffee ice cream, slightly softened
Serious Chocolate Sauce (page 176), Lighter
    Chocolate Sauce (page 176), or
    store-bought chocolate sauce

1. Chill a 1½-quart metal mold or bowl, then oil it and line it with plastic wrap, leaving an overhang to make unmolding easy. Pack the chocolate ice cream into the mold, spreading it evenly with a small offset spatula. Freeze for at least 30 minutes, or until firm.

2. Pack the vanilla ice cream into the mold, spreading it evenly. Freeze for at least 30 minutes, or until firm.

3. Pack the coffee ice cream into the mold, spreading it evenly. Freeze, tightly wrapped, until firm, at least 6 hours, or up to 3 weeks.

4. Up to 6 hours before serving, unmold the bombe onto a chilled serving platter. Tightly cover and return to the freezer until ready to serve.

5. To serve, remove the bombe from the freezer and let stand for 10 to 15 minutes. Cut into slices with a knife dipped in hot water and wiped clean before each cut. Drizzle with the sauce, and pass additional sauce at the table.

TWO-LAYER ICE CREAM BOMBE

You might top the layer of raspberry sauce with crushed Praline (page xxxix).

SERVES 4 TO 6

1 pint vanilla ice cream, slightly softened
Raspberry Sauce (page 187)
1 pint raspberry sorbet, slightly softened

1. Chill a 1-quart metal mold or bowl, then oil it and line it with plastic wrap, leaving an overhang to make unmolding easy. Pack the vanilla ice cream into the mold, spreading it evenly with a small offset spatula. Freeze for at least 30 minutes, or until firm.

2. Spread a thin layer of the sauce over the ice cream, going all the way to the edges. Freeze for at least 30 minutes, or until firm.

3. Pack the raspberry sorbet into the mold, spreading it evenly with the spatula. Freeze, tightly wrapped, until firm, at least 4 hours, or up to 3 weeks.

4. Up to 6 hours before serving, unmold the bombe onto a chilled serving platter. Tightly cover and return to the freezer until ready to serve.

5. To serve, remove the bombe from the freezer and let stand for 10 to 15 minutes. Cut into slices with a knife dipped in hot water and wiped clean before each cut. Drizzle with some of the remaining sauce, and pass additional sauce at the table.

INDIVIDUAL SORBET-AND-ICE-CREAM BOMBES

Another wonderfully easy but impressive make-ahead dessert. You can layer these in muffin cups or popover pans, brioche molds, small bowls, custard cups or old china teacups, ramekins, tiny cake pans, barquettes, or oval, heart-, leaf-, or pyramid-shaped molds. Serve on chilled plates in a pool of the sauce. You might also use just one flavor of ice cream or sorbet—molded lemon sorbet served with raspberry sauce and garnished with fresh blueberries would be just the thing.

serves 4

1 pint chocolate sorbet, slightly softened
1 pint vanilla ice cream, slightly softened
Chocolate Raspberry Sauce (page 177), Lighter
    Chocolate Sauce (page 176), or store-bought
    chocolate sauce

1. Chill four individual molds, then line with plastic wrap, leaving an overhang to make unmolding easy. Pack the chocolate sorbet into the molds, spreading it evenly and filling the molds about half full. Freeze for at least 30 minutes, or until firm.

2. Pack the vanilla ice cream into the molds, spreading it evenly. Freeze, tightly wrapped, until firm, at least 2 hours, or up to 2 weeks.

3. Up to 2 hours before serving, unmold the bombes. Tightly cover and return to the freezer until ready to serve.

4. To serve, transfer the bombes to the refrigerator for 5 minutes or so. Drizzle four chilled serving plates with the sauce and top with the bombes. Pass additional sauce at the table.

FLAVOR INSPIRATIONS
for bombes

Vanilla ice cream, a thin layer of crushed gingersnaps, and butter brickle ice cream; or butter pecan ice cream, a layer of crushed toffee, and Heath bar crunch ice cream

Vanilla ice cream, pineapple sorbet, and strawberry ice cream, with Sliced Strawberry Topping (page 188)

Vanilla ice cream, a layer of store-bought lemon curd and crumbled meringue, and lemon ice cream

Vanilla ice cream, gelato, and sorbet, with any chocolate, fruit, or berry sauce

Vanilla, chocolate, and peppermint ice cream (a classic)

Chocolate ice cream, a thin layer of sweetened chestnut puree, and vanilla ice cream, with any chocolate sauce and a garnish of candied chestnuts

Bittersweet chocolate, milk chocolate, and white chocolate ice cream, with Chocolate Raspberry Sauce (page 177) or any chocolate sauce

Strawberry, pistachio, and white chocolate ice cream

Strawberry and orange ice cream, with Strawberries Romanoff (page 148)

Coffee and vanilla ice cream, with a thin layer of chopped dried plums steeped in Armagnac

Peach ice cream and peach sorbet, with Raspberry Sauce (page 187)

Praline and strawberry ice cream, with a layer of Praline Powder (page xxxix)

Lemon ice cream and raspberry sorbet

Praline and pumpkin ice cream

Coffee and burnt almond ice cream; chocolate, caramel, and coffee ice cream; or chocolate, coffee, and hazelnut gelato or ice cream

Peach, strawberry, and rose petal gelato or ice cream

Raspberry gelato and raspberry sorbet, with Blueberry Sauce (page 185); or raspberry sorbet, vanilla ice cream, and mango sorbet, with Raspberry Sauce (page 187)

Mango, coconut, and pineapple sorbet, with Passion Fruit Syrup (page 206)

Orange sorbet and vanilla ice cream, with orange segments tossed with Caramel Syrup (page 199)

Apricot sorbet and vanilla ice cream, with Warm Chocolate Sauce (page 175) flavored with a little green Chartreuse

Mango, lemon, and raspberry sorbet

Raspberry sorbet, Praline Powder (page xxxix), and vanilla ice cream; or raspberry sorbet, vanilla ice cream, and strawberry sorbet

Peach sorbet, vanilla ice cream, and cassis sorbet; or peach sorbet, chocolate ice cream, and orange sorbet

Apricot sorbet, a layer of toasted sliced almonds, and vanilla ice cream

garnish options for bombes

- Chocolate curls (see page xxxviii)
- Candied violets
- Crushed cookies
- Nuts
- Praline Powder (page xxxix)
- Crushed candies
- Toasted sweetened shredded coconut
- Toasted slivered almonds
- Chocolate nibs (page xxxix)

The microwave can be a great tool for streamlining your ice cream dessert preparation.

- Use the microwave to defrost ice cream before preparing an ice cream dessert. The defrost setting works best. Sorbets generally take less time to soften than ice creams.
- One of the things the microwave does best is melt chocolate. Finely chop the chocolate and put it in a microwave-safe bowl; don't cover it. Microwave on low power for small increments of time, and keep in mind that it won't look melted until it's stirred.
- To peel peaches easily, first microwave each for 30 seconds or so.
- Melt the butter for the crusts for ice cream pies in the microwave.
- Bake cookie crumb crusts for ice cream pies in glass pie plates in the microwave—it takes just a couple of minutes. Set the timer for 2 minutes. Check the crust, then zap it for 30-second intervals as needed. Let cool.
- Reheat sauces and syrups in seconds in the microwave; use low power.

microwave chocolate-dipped strawberries

You might also use this to dip beautiful pieces of glazed or dried fruit—try peaches, nectarines, apricots, and pineapple.

serves 2 TO 4

3 ounces bittersweet, semisweet, milk, or white chocolate, finely chopped
1½ teaspoons flavorless vegetable oil
1 pint ripe strawberries, preferably on the stem

1. Stir together the chocolate and oil in a 1-cup glass measure. Microwave on high power for 10 to 15 seconds, then stir until smooth. If the chocolate is not completely melted, continue to microwave it in 5-second increments until it is smooth when you stir.

2. Line a baking sheet with wax paper. Wipe off the strawberries, but do not wash or hull them. Holding the stem or hull, dip each berry into the chocolate so that about three-quarters of it is covered with chocolate. Shake any excess chocolate back into the glass measure, and place the strawberry on the baking sheet. Refrigerate for 30 minutes before serving.

5

FROZEN MOMENTS: SANDWICHES, POPS, AND CONES

● ● ● ● ● ○ ○ ○

Ice cream sandwiches are a perennial hit with people of any age. Your favorite cookies, large or small, can be filled with ice cream, frozen yogurt, gelato, and/or sorbet and placed in the freezer for a serve-anytime dessert. Use any kind of cookies or cookie substitutes—store-bought, slice-and-bake cookies, small thin meringues, thin slices of pound cake cut into circles, or your own homemade cookies. Try different cookies with different kinds of ice cream and experiment with garnishes to find your favorite combinations. Mix and match to your heart's content.

Soften the frozen desserts (you may not need to soften sorbet for as long as ice cream or gelato) before making the sandwiches, but don't let them start to melt. Melted ice cream could soften the cookies and become icy when it freezes again. If the ice cream is too hard, though, the cookies might break. Soften the ice cream in the refrigerator for 10 to 15 minutes, or microwave it for a couple of minutes on defrost.

For easy assembly, you can freeze the ice cream or sorbet in 6- or 12-ounce frozen juice containers. Unmold, cut into slices with a warm knife, and place each slice between 2 cookies.

If it's hot in your kitchen, freeze the cookies first, to keep the ice cream from melting, and place each sandwich in the freezer as soon as you make it. Then wrap each sandwich in plastic wrap, place in a freezer container, and cover tightly. You can keep the sandwiches frozen for up to 1 week. If you'd like, dip the sandwiches in melted bittersweet, semisweet, milk, or white chocolate. Dip only about one-third to one-half of each sandwich; if completely coated in chocolate, they're difficult to eat. You can make decorative patterns in the chocolate with a fork. Then firm up the sandwiches in the freezer before serving.

If you use large cookies, you might cut the sandwiches into halves or quarters before serving.

Another serving option is to place the sandwiches in bowls and pour sauce over them, and/or serve a pitcher of sauce at the table—they're great with warm sauces. Serving them with sauce definitely lifts them into the realm of not just kid stuff.

ice cream sandwiches

Soften the ice cream just until it can be spread; don't let it melt. On a warm summer day, you can probably use it directly from the freezer. If it's really hot outside, freeze the cookies first and put each sandwich in the freezer immediately after it's assembled. You will need more or less ice cream depending on the size of your cookies. Serve with individual or communal pitchers of hot fudge, chocolate, fruit, butterscotch, or caramel sauce.

MAKES 4 SANDWICHES

About 1 pint vanilla ice cream, slightly softened
8 soft Dutch cocoa cookies (each about 3½ inches in diameter)

1. Spread about ⅓ cup of the ice cream over the bottom of one cookie and top with another cookie, right side up; gently press the cookies together. Repeat with the remaining cookies and ice cream.

2. Serve immediately, or freeze, tightly wrapped, for up to 1 week.

FLAVOR
INSPIRATIONS

Other favorite combinations: Chocolate wafers with coconut or raspberry sorbet or mint chocolate chip or chocolate raspberry truffle ice cream; graham crackers and lemon ice cream; gingersnaps with triple caramel chunk ice cream; oatmeal cookies with rum raisin, Heath bar crunch, or peach ice cream; chocolate chip cookies with coffee gelato; molasses cookies with dulce de leche or almond ice cream; Dutch apple cookies with caramel apple gelato; coconut cookies with mango or passion fruit ice cream; and peanut butter cookies with dark chocolate ice cream.

Not necessary, but dazzling and divine: Roll the sides of the sandwiches in miniature chocolate chips, toasted coconut, crushed candies or cookies, chopped toasted nuts, sprinkles, or whatever suits your fancy. Just spread the goodies on a plate and roll each sandwich to coat the sides.

Brioche ice cream sandwiches

If you lived in Sicily, you might have these for breakfast in the summertime. Hmmm, is that a good enough reason to move? You don't have to use the very rich eggy and buttery French brioche; you could use a soft roll, more typical of the Italian version. You'll use more or less gelato depending on the size of your brioche. Just don't fill them so full that they're totally messy.

MAKES 4 SANDWICHES

1 pint coffee gelato, slightly softened
4 individual brioche, split horizontally

Spread about ⅓ cup of the gelato over the bottom half of 1 brioche and add the top half, right side up; gently press the brioche together. Repeat with the remaining gelato and brioche. Serve immediately.

FLAVOR INSPIRATIONS

Ice cream, frozen yogurt, gelato, and sorbet: Instead of coffee, try caramel, chocolate, chocolate hazelnut, coffee, pistachio, strawberry, tiramisù, vanilla, coconut, ginger, or raspberry. Or try lemon, coffee, or chocolate sorbet.

croissant ice cream sandwiches

If you have a choice, buy all-butter croissants. If you'd like to gild the lily, serve whipped cream on the side.

MAKES 4 SANDWICHES

4 croissants, split horizontally
1 to 2 pints vanilla ice cream, slightly softened
Serious Chocolate Sauce (page 176), Warm or Cool
    Chocolate Sauce (page 175), or store-bought
    chocolate sauce
Unsweetened cocoa powder for dusting, optional

1. Position a rack in the middle of the oven and preheat the oven to 350 degrees F.

2. Toast the croissants right on the oven rack until the cut edges are just beginning to brown.

3. Arrange the croissant bottoms on four serving plates. Top them with scoops of the ice cream, about 2 tablespoons each of the chocolate sauce, and the croissant tops, set at a slight angle. Lightly dust with cocoa powder, if using, and serve immediately. Pass additional sauce at the table.

POUND CAKE ICE CREAM SANDWICHES

My mom used to serve tiny sandwiches made with a Pullman loaf that she sliced horizontally and spread with different colors and flavors of cream cheese to members of her bridge club. These ice cream sandwiches are modeled after those tea sandwiches. Cut them any way you'd like—try triangles or rounds, or use heart- or star-shaped cookie cutters.

MAKES 16 SMALL SANDWICHES

One 10¾-ounce store-bought frozen pound cake, thawed

1 pint vanilla ice cream, slightly softened

1. Remove just the top crust from the pound cake (about ¼ inch) with a long serrated knife. Carefully cut the cake horizontally into six ¼-inch-thick layers.

2. Using a small offset spatula, spread the bottom cake layer evenly with about ½ cup of the ice cream (don't mound it in the center). Add another layer of cake and top it with another even layer of about ½ cup ice cream. Top with a third layer of cake. Wrap tightly in plastic wrap and then in aluminum foil and place in the freezer. Repeat with the remaining cake and ice cream. Freeze for at least 2 hours, or up to 1 week.

3. To serve, transfer the filled cake layers to a cutting board. Cut each one crosswise into eight ¾-inch-thick slices. Arrange the sandwiches on a chilled platter, and serve immediately.

FLAVOR
INSPIRATIONS

Ice cream, frozen yogurt, and gelato: Instead of vanilla, try orange blossom special, pistachio, cherry vanilla, chocolate, coffee, lemon, caramel, ginger, hazelnut, mango, butter brickle, peach, rose petal, strawberry, tiramisù, mixed berry, raspberry and cream, raspberry lemon cooler, Key lime pie, or fraises de bois ice cream. Or use one layer of vanilla and one of sorbet. Also give lemon, chocolate, raspberry, strawberry, coconut, orange, apricot, cherry, lime, mango, passion fruit, or peach sorbet a try.

Everyone loves a Popsicle or an ice cream bar—eating one makes you feel like a kid again. They're fun for an adult dinner party, served upside down in elegant bowls, with the flavors layered, swirled, rippled, and/or two-tone. With store-bought gelato, sorbet, ice cream, and frozen yogurt, in any combination, perhaps with a flavored syrup swirled in, the possibilities are endless. Make your own Creamsicles (if you are from the West Coast, you called them 50/50 bars), using Tahitian vanilla gelato and blood orange sorbet—even better than those from your childhood.

Making your own Popsicles—or "ice lollies," as they're called in England—couldn't be easier. Use any kind of mold, from store-bought Popsicle molds to wax paper cups or yogurt containers to candy molds or small fluted gelatin molds; just make sure that they are deep enough to secure the stick. There are advantages to molding them in small cups—namely that you can put them back in the cup between bites to catch any melt, leaving just a bit to sip at the end.

Popsicle molds come in many sizes. Whatever the size, fill the molds almost full, leaving a little room for expansion when frozen, add the sticks or handles, and freeze for at least four hours, or overnight. If you don't have sticks or handles, use sturdy plastic spoons. To unmold, hold under warm running water for about five seconds—carefully, so you don't melt them—and then twist the handles and lift out the Popsicles.

marbleized lollies

To ripple the flavors and colors, use sharply contrasting colors. Fill your molds with alternate spoonfuls of softened ice cream and flavored syrup, half sorbet and half frozen yogurt, or your choice. Use a skewer to gently swirl them together.

high-contrast striped pops

Layer the flavors in stripes, however many you want, letting each layer freeze solid before adding the next.

california sunset pops

There's something most refreshing and fine-looking about these. Use sorbets in shades of pink, red, and orange (such as pink lemonade, raspberry, strawberry, blood orange, apricot, cherry, mango, peach, passion fruit, tangerine, cranberry, orange, or watermelon). Try layering them from the darkest to the lightest in the molds.

ice cream brain-freeze headaches

If you eat ice cream really quickly, the cold ice cream touching the back of your palate causes blood vessels that go to the brain to constrict. This can cause a sharp pain, though it rarely lasts more than a minute. The cure? Either eat a bit slower, or savor the ice cream on your tongue longer to warm it a bit.

kids' corner

Have you ever seen a child experience her first taste of ice cream? I have, and I'll never forget it. Little Maeve Moran tasted chocolate ice cream at her first birthday party, and immediately tried to eat the bowl. She didn't waste a split second wondering if she liked it or not—she *knew*. Ice cream is a favorite part of childhood, one that hardly needs enhancing, but some treats are more kid-friendly than others. Here are some:

- Thread marshmallows and strawberries or chunks of banana alternately on skewers, toast them over an open flame, and serve with ice cream and chocolate sauce.
- Pour marshmallow sauce over chocolate ice cream and top with chocolate-flavored malted milk powder and a cherry garnish.
- Grind chocolate chip cookies into coarse crumbs. Roll balls of ice cream—using rocky road is fun—in the crumbs, and serve topped with chocolate sauce.
- Fold together canned cherries and marshmallow cream and use as a sauce for brownie sundaes.
- Serve ice cream in tiny flowerpots lined with foil cups. Top with sprinkles and a fresh flower (unsprayed and nontoxic, of course) in the middle of each.

- Blend milk, a favorite ice cream, and a banana for a special milkshake; or use strawberries or peaches instead of the banana.
- Paint waffle cones with chocolate and dip in nuts, crushed candies, or cookies.
- For Halloween, make witches' hats: Brush sugar cones with warm melted chocolate, coating them completely, and let set. Fill the cones with chocolate ice cream and serve on a cookie in a bowl, point up. Add a witch's face to the ice cream with gumdrops, if you'd like.
- Garnish sundaes and drinks with dried fruit leather or roll-ups.

Dylan's Candy Bar in Manhattan serves a "Central Park Sundae" that any kid, big or little, would love. They top a favorite ice cream with hot fudge sauce and animal crackers.

My tongue is smiling.

✳

—ABIGAIL TRILLIN, AGE FOUR, AFTER EATING CHOCOLATE ICE CREAM;
FROM CALVIN TRILLIN, *ALICE, LET'S EAT*

Recipes for ice cream cones may seem a little silly in a book about what to do with store-bought ice cream, but I've included one recipe because they are so easy and rewarding to make at home. Ways to doctor up store-bought cones are included here too. Use any store-bought cones—cake cones, rainbow cones, sugar cones, or Oreo cones.

If you want to make your own sugar cones, you'll need a special pizzelle iron. All you do is pour the batter on the round waffle griddle and cook it, then twist the wafer around a conical form that comes with the machine. The irons sell for about fifty dollars and most kitchenware shops carry them; they are also available online from the Chef's Catalog, www.chefscatalog.com, or call 800-342-3255. On the other hand, Sur la Table (www.surlatable.com or 800-243-0852) offers fun ice cream dishes that look like cones and can be reused.

Don't hesitate to serve these to grown-up guests. Everyone loves an ice cream cone. There's something playful and lighthearted about them, but they can look sophisticated and quite stunning served upside down in beautiful bowls.

roll-your-own sugar cones

Known as pizzelle *(pronounced "peet-sellay"), these are quick and easy to make, as long as you have a special iron. But you don't have to make cones with these; they can also be cut into quarters and used as wafers. Simply stick them into the ice cream, pointed end down. You can also mold the pizzelle over an inverted bowl, ramekin, or custard cup to form a* tulipe, *or cup, for filling with ice cream or sorbet. Or roll them into tubes that can be served alongside an ice cream dessert or filled with ice cream using a pastry bag. Or mold them over a rolling pin or tall drinking glass on its side to form* tuiles *for serving with ice cream. Or use them—carefully—to make ice cream sandwiches.*

A note on making cones: I set the dial on number 3 for cooking and cook my pizzelle longer than the manufacturer's directions indicate, because I like them a uniform golden brown, not a pale color.

You can make smaller pizzelle using 1 tablespoon batter for each. Use these to make tubes, tuiles, *cookies for ice cream sandwiches, or wafers.*

MAKES 8 CONES

3 large egg whites
¾ cup confectioners' sugar
½ cup all-purpose flour
Pinch of salt
6 tablespoons (¾ stick) unsalted butter,
    melted and cooled
½ teaspoon pure vanilla extract

1. Lightly oil the pizzelle iron and preheat it according to the manufacturer's instructions.

2. Whisk together the egg whites, sugar, flour, and salt in a medium bowl just until well combined; the mixture will be lumpy. Whisk in the butter and vanilla until smooth.

3. Place a generous 2 tablespoons of the batter in the center of the pizzelle iron, close the iron, and cook for about 1½ minutes, or according to the manufacturer's directions, until golden brown. Working quickly, remove the hot pizzelle from the iron with a fork and place it on a soft kitchen towel. Immediately position the point of the cone form about ½ inch from the edge of the pizzelle and use the towel to help you roll it around the mold to form a cone, then let the towel fall away. Hold the cone together until it stays in shape; while it is still warm, pinch the bottom point together to seal it tightly. When cool, remove the form from the cone. Repeat with the remaining batter. The cones can be stored in an airtight container at room temperature for up to 1 week.

chocolate-dipped ice cream cones

The amounts given here are for standard-sized sugar cones. If you use oversized cones, you'll need up to twice the chocolate and nuts. Try bittersweet chocolate with chopped toasted hazelnuts, milk chocolate with toasted sliced almonds, or white chocolate with chopped pistachios. Instead of nuts, you might use miniature chocolate or butterscotch chips, sprinkles, chopped toffee or toffee bits, grated chocolate, or crushed cookies and/or candies. Dip the cones in bittersweet chocolate and sprinkle with grated white chocolate (or vice versa). You can also melt an extra bit of chocolate and brush the interiors of the cones with it.

makes 12 cones

½ cup semisweet chocolate chips or 3 ounces bittersweet or semisweet chocolate, finely chopped
⅓ cup finely chopped toasted nuts
12 sugar cones

1. Melt the chocolate in a heatproof bowl set over a saucepan of simmering water, stirring until smooth. Transfer to a small shallow bowl.

2. Place the nuts on a sheet of wax paper.

3. Hold a cone upside down and dip it into the melted chocolate, coating the top ½ inch or so; shake off any excess. Roll the coated part of the cone in the chopped nuts. Place the cone in a short glass, pointed end down, or lay it on wax paper for about 10 minutes, until the chocolate sets. Repeat with the remaining cones.

4. Use the cones immediately, or store in an airtight container at cool room temperature for up to 1 week.

CHOCOLATE-DIPPED ICE-CREAM-FILLED CONES

The previous recipe is for coating cones with chocolate; this is for dipping ice cream cones into chocolate. Dip just the ice cream scoop, or dip a smidgen of the cone as well. You can add a teaspoon or two of instant espresso powder to the melted chocolate. Before the chocolate coating sets, roll the scoop in chopped nuts, crushed candies or cookies, coconut, or whatever you have your heart set on. Toffee bits are quite wonderful. Here's a chance to make your own "Nutty Buddies" with good chocolate and fine ice cream.

makes 8 cones

8 sugar cones
1 to 2 pints vanilla ice cream, slightly softened
9 ounces bittersweet or semisweet chocolate,
    finely chopped
2 tablespoons flavorless vegetable oil

1. Using a small spoon, partially fill each cone with ice cream (be gentle). Scoop a large ball of the ice cream onto the cone, pressing gently to anchor it, and place the cone, ice cream side up, in a small glass. Freeze for at least 2 hours, or up to overnight.
2. Melt the chocolate with the oil in a heatproof bowl set over a saucepan of simmering water, stirring until smooth. Transfer to a 1-cup glass measure.

3. Working quickly, dip the ice cream end of 1 cone into the chocolate, rotating it to coat completely. Gently shake off any excess chocolate, return the cone to the glass, and place in the freezer. Repeat with the remaining cones and chocolate. Freeze for at least 1 hour before serving. The cones can be prepared up to 1 week ahead; once they are frozen, wrap each cone tightly in plastic wrap and store in self-sealing plastic bags.

In trying to make wise and correct decisions about the ice cream cone in your hand, you should always keep the objectives in mind. The main objective, of course, is to get the cone under control. Secondarily, one will want to eat the cone calmly and with pleasure. Real pleasure lies not simply in eating the cone but in eating it right. Let us assume you have darted to your open space [reference to dripping-problem areas] and made your necessary emergency repairs. The cone is still dangerous—still, so to speak, "live." But you can now proceed with it in an orderly fashion. First, revolve the cone through the full three hundred and sixty degrees, snapping at the loose gobs of ice cream; turn the cone by moving the thumb away from you and the forefinger toward you, so the cone moves counterclockwise. Then, with the cone still "wound," which will require the wrist to be bent at the full right angle toward you, apply pressure with the mouth and tongue to accomplish overall realignment, straightening and settling the whole mess. Then, unwinding the cone back through three hundred and sixty degrees, remove any trickles of ice cream. From here on, some supplementary repairs may be necessary, but the cone is now defused.

—L. Rust Hills in the August 24, 1968, issue of *The New Yorker,*
quoted in Paul Dickson, *The Great American Ice Cream Book*

6

JUST ADD Ice Cream: Bases for Easy and Incredible Ice Cream Delights

CHOCOLATE CUPS

Fill these simple but sophisticated cups with your favorite ice cream, gelato, and/or sorbet; each one will hold ⅓ to ½ cup. If you don't have room for a muffin tin in your freezer, after the chocolate has set slightly, just put the foil cups themselves in the freezer. Make sure the chocolate coating is thick and sturdy; if it's thin, the cups will be delicate and break easily. Feel free to double or triple the recipe. If you'd like, sprinkle the ice cream with crushed candies or cookies, or drizzle with a sauce or syrup before serving.

MAKES 4 CUPS

½ cup semisweet chocolate chips or 3 ounces
    bittersweet or semisweet chocolate, finely
    chopped
1½ teaspoons unsalted butter or flavorless
    vegetable oil
1 pint vanilla ice cream

1. Melt the chocolate with the butter in a heat-proof bowl set over a saucepan of simmering water, stirring until smooth. Remove from heat.

2. Place four fluted foil baking cups in a muffin pan. Starting from the top, spoon the chocolate down the sides of each cup, using 3 to 4 teaspoons per cup to cover the entire inside; use a brush to spread the chocolate over the sides and bottoms of the cups, then spread it from the bottom back up the sides to reinforce the sides. Freeze the cups for at least 15 minutes, or until the chocolate is set.

3. Remove 1 cup at a time from the freezer and, with cool hands, in a cool room, gently and quickly peel the foil baking cup from the chocolate. If the chocolate starts to melt while you're peeling the baking cup off, pop the cup back into the freezer for a minute or two before you give it another try. Transfer the chocolate cups to a chilled platter and refrigerate. (These can be frozen in a self-sealing plastic bag for several weeks.)

4. Up to 1 hour before serving, working with 1 cup at a time, scoop the ice cream into the chocolate cups. Freeze until ready to serve.

Ice cream, frozen yogurt, and gelato: Instead of vanilla, try cinnamon, Black Forest, ginger, chocolate orange, green tea, vanilla caramel fudge, caramel, chocolate hazelnut, dulce de leche, butter brickle, chocolate raspberry truffle, coffee, peanut butter truffle, coconut, tiramisù, or any berry or other fruit ice cream. Or try chocolate rainbow, cassis, strawberry, raspberry, mango, lemon, cherry, peach, chocolate, coconut, passion fruit, pear, or blood orange sorbet.

Not necessary, but dazzling and divine: Drizzle with chocolate sauce, caramel sauce, or any berry or other fruit sauce. Garnish with strawberries or cherries on the stem; Microwave Chocolate-Dipped Strawberries (page 116); cocoa nibs (see page xxxix); crushed cookies, candies, or Praline (page xxxix); or toasted nuts.

TULIPES AND TUILES

These delicate cookie shells can be shaped like a tulip or a French roof tile. To make tulipes, *you shape the hot cookies over an inverted ramekin, custard cup, or glass to make a wavy flower shape—they make lovely edible containers for servings of ice cream. To make* tuiles, *you just drape the hot cookies over a rolling pin and leave them there until they have cooled. They have a graceful, pleasing shape that makes a beautiful garnish on a plate of ice cream and/or sorbet.*

MAKES 12 TULIPES OR TUILES

3 large egg whites
¾ cup confectioners' sugar
½ cup all-purpose flour
¼ teaspoon salt
6 tablespoons (¾ stick) unsalted butter,
    melted and cooled
½ teaspoon pure vanilla extract

1. Preheat the oven to 350 degrees F. Generously butter a baking sheet. Set out four glasses (they should be about 2 inches in diameter at the base) or custard cups, turned upside down, if making *tulipes*, or set out a rolling pin if making *tuiles*.

2. Whisk together the egg whites, sugar, flour, and salt in a medium bowl just until well combined; the mixture will be lumpy. Whisk in the butter and vanilla until smooth.

3. Drop 1 tablespoon of the batter onto the baking sheet. Repeat to make 4 cookies, spacing them about 3 inches apart. With a small offset spatula, spread each cookie into a 4-inch round.

4. Bake the cookies for 5 to 7 minutes, until the edges are golden brown. With a wide metal spatula, quickly transfer a cookie to an inverted glass, letting it drape over the sides, or drape over the rolling pin. Let cool. Repeat with the remaining cookies on the baking sheet. If the cookies become too hard to shape, return the baking sheet to the oven to soften them slightly.

5. Repeat with the remaining batter. Store the cookies in a tightly covered container or self-sealing plastic bag for up to 1 week.

shortcakes

Don't bake these more than an hour ahead—they are best made at the last minute. Serve with Caramel Apples (page 163), Strawberries and Basil (page 147), Sliced Strawberry Topping (page 188), Cherry Compote with Balsamic Vinegar (page 152), Warm Mango and Basil Compote (page 156), or your favorite fruit topping—with your choice of ice cream and/or sorbet.

makes 6 shortcakes

1¾ cups all-purpose flour

3 tablespoons sugar, plus more for sprinkling

1 tablespoon baking powder

Pinch of salt

1½ teaspoons finely grated lemon zest

1 cup chilled heavy cream, plus more cream or
    milk for brushing

1 teaspoon pure vanilla extract

2 pints vanilla ice cream

Topping of your choice

1. Position a rack in the middle of the oven and preheat the oven to 425 degrees F. Butter a large baking sheet.

2. Sift together the flour, sugar, baking powder, and salt into a bowl. Stir in the zest with a fork.

3. In a large bowl, combine the cream and vanilla extract. Beat the cream with an electric mixer on medium-high speed just until it holds soft peaks when the beaters are lifted. Make a well in the center of the flour mixture, add the whipped cream, and stir with a fork just until the mixture forms a dough.

4. Knead the dough on a lightly floured surface about 6 times, or just until well combined. Roll or pat out the dough ½ inch thick. Cut out a total of 6 rounds with a 4-inch cutter, gathering the scraps and rerolling. Brush the rounds with cream or milk and sprinkle with sugar. Arrange the shortcakes on the baking sheet.

5. Bake the shortcakes for 12 to 15 minutes, or until golden brown. Transfer with a spatula to a wire rack and let cool.

6. To serve, split each shortcake in half, arrange 2 halves on each of six plates, and serve with the ice cream and the topping.

Check out www.everythingicecream.com for ice-cream-related gift items—jewelry, stationery, dishes, ice cream scoops, Christmas ornaments, magnets, candles, even clothing. Or go to www.IceCreamSource.com for premium brands of ice cream from all over the country, ice cream cakes, dairy-free and kosher products, sauces, Zeroll scoops, soda glasses, banana split and sundae dishes, apparel, and books.

sweet tortillas

Here's an idea I got from Good Housekeeping, *my favorite food magazine. In the test kitchen these were cut into wedges, and you can do that too, but give this version a try. You can make them up to a week ahead; store in self-sealing plastic bags, and warm gently before serving. I use a scalloped round biscuit cutter; you could also use a star- or heart-shaped cookie cutter. Arrange the tortillas on plates and top with ice cream—dulce de leche is a grand choice. Or layer small scoops of ice cream between three layers of tortillas for a tortilla "Napoleon."*

SERVES 4 TO 6

2 tablespoons light or dark brown sugar
Pinch of ground cinnamon
Two 9½-inch flour tortillas
2 tablespoons unsalted butter, melted

1. Position a rack in the middle of the oven and preheat the oven to 375 degrees F.
2. Stir together the sugar and cinnamon in a small bowl. Cut 6 rounds from each tortilla with a 3-inch round biscuit cutter, preferably with a scalloped edge. Arrange the tortilla rounds on a large nonstick baking sheet, brush with the butter, and sprinkle evenly with the sugar mixture.
3. Bake for 10 to 12 minutes, until golden brown. Serve warm, or cool completely on the baking sheet on a wire rack, then store in a self-sealing plastic bag or airtight container at room temperature for up to 1 week; reheat in a low oven before serving.

profiteroles

Making profiteroles is a process like no other I know, and I'd love to know who made the first batch of the dough, called pâté choux, *and whether it was accidental or intentional. My preference is to fill the profiteroles with coffee ice cream. You might try raspberry ice cream with Chocolate Raspberry Sauce (page 177).*

serves 4

½ cup all-purpose flour

2 tablespoons unsweetened cocoa powder

3 tablespoons unsalted butter

1 tablespoon granulated sugar

Pinch of salt

2 large eggs

¾ cup vanilla ice cream

Confectioners' sugar for dusting

Serious Chocolate Sauce (page 176) or
    store-bought chocolate sauce, warmed

1. Position a rack in the middle of the oven and preheat the oven to 400 degrees F. Butter a large baking sheet.

2. Sift the flour and cocoa powder together into a small bowl. Bring 6 tablespoons water, the butter, granulated sugar, and salt to a boil in a medium heavy saucepan over high heat, stirring until the butter is melted. Remove the pan from the heat, add the flour mixture all at once, and stir until the mixture pulls away from the sides of the pan, forming a ball.

3. Transfer the mixture to a large bowl and, with an electric mixer on high speed, beat in the eggs one at a time, beating well after each addition and scraping down the sides of the bowl as necessary. Continue beating until the dough is smooth, dry looking, and cooled to room temperature.

4. Drop the dough by slightly rounded tablespoonfuls onto the baking sheet, forming 12 tall mounds, and smooth each with damp fingers.

5. Bake for 20 to 25 minutes, until puffed and crisp. Let cool on a wire rack. (The profiteroles can be baked 1 day in advance and stored in an airtight container at room temperature. Reheat on a baking sheet in a preheated 375 degree F oven for 5 minutes, or until crisp again, then let cool on a rack before proceeding with the recipe.)

6. Cut each profiterole in half crosswise with a serrated knife; discard any uncooked dough in the centers. Place about 1 tablespoon of the ice cream in the bottom of each profiterole, cover with the tops, and lightly sift confectioners' sugar over them. Pour about ¼ cup of the chocolate sauce onto each of four dessert plates, and arrange 3 profiteroles on each plate. Serve immediately.

TOASTED ANGEL FOOD CAKE AND ICE CREAM

If angel food loaf cakes are not available to you, just use slices from a traditional round cake. Don't limit yourself to the strawberry combination here—use other fruits like peach, raspberry, blueberry, apricot, or plum, or try another whole flavor set, such as chocolate, caramel, or butterscotch.

serves 8

1 store-bought angel food loaf cake (about 7 × 3 inches)
2 pints strawberry ice cream or strawberry sorbet (or 1 pint of each)
Sliced Strawberry Topping (page 188)
Slightly Sweetened Whipped Cream (page 209), optional
Toasted sliced almonds, optional

1. Cut the cake into 8 slices. Lightly toast the slices in a toaster or toaster oven.

2. Arrange the cake slices on serving plates and top each with small scoops of the ice cream and the strawberry topping. Garnish each serving with a dollop of the whipped cream and some of the toasted almonds, if using. Serve immediately.

Ice cream was just as good when they only had three flavors: vanilla, chocolate, and strawberry.

✳

—ANDY ROONEY, *CURMUDGEON*

toasted Brioche and ice cream

You could use small individual brioches or halved larger ones instead of slices from a loaf. Warm Cherry Sauce (page 191) is also superb with this.

serves 4

Four ¾-inch-thick slices brioche

1 to 2 pints vanilla ice cream

Old-fashioned Caramel Sauce (page 181), or one of the variations, or store-bought caramel sauce, warmed

Slightly Sweetened Whipped Cream (page 209), optional

Chopped toasted pecans, optional

1. Preheat the broiler. Arrange the brioche slices on a sheet of aluminum foil on the broiler pan and broil 3 to 4 inches from the heat for 1 to 2 minutes, or until golden brown and well toasted; rotate the pan if necessary for even browning. Turn the slices over and broil for 1 to 2 minutes longer, or until golden brown and well toasted.

2. Arrange the brioche on four serving plates, top each with small scoops of the ice cream, and drizzle with the caramel sauce. Top each serving with a dollop of the whipped cream and toasted pecans, if using.

TOASTED POUND CAKE AND ICE CREAM

As an alternative to broiling, you can bake the pound cake right on the oven rack in a 450 degree F oven for about five minutes, or toast it in a toaster or even on an outdoor grill, if you happen to have it fired up. Watch the slices carefully, as different pound cakes toast in different amounts of time; I like them nice and dark. Top the slices with vanilla ice cream and just about any syrup or sauce you have on hand.

serves 4

Four ¾-inch-thick slices homemade or
store-bought pound cake
1 to 2 pints vanilla ice cream
Warm Chocolate Sauce (page 175) or
Old-fashioned Caramel Sauce (page 181)

1. Preheat the broiler. Arrange the pound cake on a sheet of aluminum foil on the broiler pan and broil 3 to 4 inches from the heat for 1 to 2 minutes, until golden brown and well toasted; rotate the pan if necessary for even browning. Turn the slices over and broil for 1 to 2 minutes longer, until golden brown and well toasted.

2. Arrange the warm slices on four serving plates, and top with scoops of ice cream and a tablespoon or two of chocolate sauce each. Pass additional sauce at the table.

- Toast cinnamon raisin bread. Remove the crusts, lightly butter the slices, and cut each in half diagonally. Top with ice cream, and a sauce or syrup, if desired.
- Top shortbread wedges with ice cream or sorbet.
- Cut gingerbread or brownies into squares. Top with ice cream and a sauce, syrup, or fruit topping.
- Split sweet muffins or scones, fill with ice cream, and serve drizzled with syrup or sauce.
- Top soft ladyfingers with ice cream or gelato and a fruit topping.
- Split chocolate cupcakes in half. Arrange the bottom halves on serving plates and top each with a scoop of ice cream and the cupcake top, a bit off center. Ladle hot fudge sauce over each and garnish with whipped cream.
- Serve warm fruit turnovers from the bakery topped with scoops of ice cream.
- Top toasted frozen waffles with ice cream, a fruit topping, and whipped cream.
- Fill baked frozen puff pastry shells with ice cream and drizzle with your favorite sauce.
- Freshly made or packaged crepes are available in many supermarkets, often in the produce section. Fold the crepes into triangles and heat them in a bit of butter in a skillet. Arrange on serving plates, and top with gelato or ice cream.
- Serve puff pastry palmiers from the market warm with ice cream.
- Toast slices of panettone and serve warm topped with gelato.

7

FRUIT CONCOCTIONS: FRUIT ON THE SIDE AND ON TOP

● ● ● ● ● ● ● ○

roasted strawberries

This recipe has been adapted from Melissa Clark's The Instant Gourmet—*a brilliant little book. It's fantastic served over Toasted Pound Cake (page 143) or with Toasted Brioche (page 142).*

serves 4

1 pound small fresh strawberries, hulled

2 tablespoons Grand Marnier or other orange
    liqueur

2 tablespoons light brown sugar

1 tablespoon unsalted butter, cut into small pieces

1 to 2 pints vanilla ice cream

¼ teaspoon pure vanilla extract

Finely chopped pistachios, optional

1. Preheat the oven to 425 degrees F.

2. Arrange the strawberries in a glass or ceramic baking dish just large enough to hold them in a single layer. Drizzle with the Grand Marnier, sprinkle with the sugar, and dot with the butter. Roast the strawberries, stirring once halfway through, for 10 minutes, or until soft and fragrant.

3. Place scoops of the ice cream in four wineglasses or bowls and top with the strawberries. Stir the vanilla extract into the juices remaining in the baking dish and pour over the desserts. Sprinkle with the pistachios, if using, and serve immediately.

strawberries and basil

The macerated berries are also perfect for serving with Shortcakes (page 137), in Pavlova (page 94) or Individual Meringue Nests (page 95), or over ripe sliced cantaloupe and vanilla ice cream. Quintessential summer flavors, strawberry and basil taste even better together than separately.

serves 4

2 pints fresh strawberries, hulled and sliced

3 tablespoons finely shredded fresh basil leaves

3 tablespoons sugar, or more to taste

1 tablespoon fresh lemon juice

1 pint vanilla ice cream

1 cup strawberry sorbet

1. Stir together the strawberries, basil, sugar, and lemon juice in a medium bowl. Let stand for about 20 minutes to allow the berries to release their juices. Taste and add sugar if necessary.

2. To serve, place scoops of the ice cream and sorbet in four large stemmed glasses or bowls. Top with the strawberries, and serve immediately.

FLAVOR
INSPIRATIONS

Ice cream, frozen yogurt, and gelato: Instead of vanilla, try raspberry, strawberry, white chocolate, pistachio, strawberry cheesecake, peach, vanilla raspberry swirl, or mango.

Sorbet: Instead of strawberry, try raspberry, lemon, mango, passion fruit, margarita, or orange.

strawberries romanoff

Named for the Russian royal family by a French chef, this is an inspired dish. This is a timeless combination.

serves 4

1 pint fresh strawberries, halved or quartered
    if large
2 tablespoons fresh orange juice
2 tablespoons confectioners' sugar
1 to 2 tablespoons Grand Marnier or other
    orange liqueur
1 to 2 pints vanilla ice cream

1. Stir together the strawberries, orange juice, sugar, and Grand Marnier in a bowl. Refrigerate, tightly covered, for 1 hour.

2. To serve, scoop the ice cream into four serving bowls or glasses. Spoon the strawberries over the ice cream, drizzle with the syrup remaining in the bowl, and serve immediately.

Life is like an ice cream cone; you have to learn to lick it.

*

—CHARLES SCHULZ

roasted nectarines with caramel sauce

Serve with Praline (page xxxix) in large pieces, or sprinkle about a tablespoon of finely chopped Praline over each serving.

serves 4

5 ripe nectarines (about 2 pounds), halved
    and pitted
½ cup heavy cream
¼ cup sugar
1 teaspoon fresh lemon juice
1 to 2 pints vanilla ice cream
Fresh raspberries for garnish, optional

1. Position a rack in the middle of the oven and preheat the oven to 375 degrees F.

2. Arrange 8 of the nectarine halves, cut side up, in a glass or ceramic baking dish just large enough to hold them in a single layer. Roast them for 20 minutes, or until softened.

3. Meanwhile, chop the remaining 2 nectarine halves. Cook them in a medium nonstick skillet over medium heat, stirring frequently, for 5 minutes, or until very soft. Set aside.

4. Heat the cream in a small saucepan over medium heat just until hot. Set aside, covered, to keep warm.

5. Heat the sugar and lemon juice in a heavy medium saucepan over medium heat, stirring until it is dissolved. Increase the heat to high and bring to a boil, washing down the sides of the pan with a damp pastry brush if you see any sugar crystals on the sides. Boil, without stirring, until the caramel turns a dark golden brown, continuing to wash down the sides of the pan with the pastry brush if necessary. Immediately remove the saucepan from the heat and, being careful to avoid spatters, add the cream about 2 tablespoons at a time. Add the chopped nectarines and stir until well combined. Pour the mixture through a strainer set over a bowl, pressing hard on the solids to extract as much liquid as possible.

6. To serve, arrange 2 nectarine halves on each of four serving plates. Add scoops of the ice cream, and top each serving with about 2 tablespoons of the caramel sauce. Serve garnished with the raspberries, if using.

BROILED PINEAPPLE WITH BROWN SUGAR–BALSAMIC SAUCE

As an alternative to broiling, you can grill the pineapple slices over medium coals; the cooking time will be about the same. The sauce keeps very well; make a double or triple batch and refrigerate it, tightly covered, for up to three months. Serve it warm over ice cream or gelato with berries or other fruit. You don't need much of this flavorful sauce, just a generous tablespoon or so per serving.

serves 4

FOR THE SAUCE

¼ cup packed dark brown sugar
2 tablespoons balsamic vinegar

Eight ½-inch-thick slices ripe pineapple, cored
1 to 2 pints vanilla ice cream

1. Combine the sugar and vinegar in a small saucepan and cook over low heat, stirring constantly, until the sugar dissolves. Increase the heat to high and bring to a boil. Set aside.

2. Preheat the broiler. Broil the pineapple slices on the broiler pan, set 5 to 6 inches under the heat, for 6 minutes. Turn the pineapple slices over and cook for 6 minutes longer, or until golden brown and soft.

3. To serve, arrange 2 pineapple slices on each of four dessert plates. Top with scoops of the ice cream, drizzle with the sauce, and serve immediately.

FLAVOR
INSPIRATIONS

Ice cream, frozen yogurt, gelato, and sorbet: Instead of vanilla, try ginger, piña colada, vanilla macadamia nut, caramel praline crunch, ginger crème brûlée, toasted hazelnut crunch, or butter pecan. Or try margarita, mango, lemon, tropical, coconut, lime, passion fruit, or pineapple sorbet.

Not necessary, but dazzling and divine: Stir ⅛ teaspoon pure vanilla extract into the sauce just before serving. Garnish with toasted macadamia nuts or crumbled nut brittle.

how to cut up a pineapple

Using a chef's knife, remove the leaves and about 1 inch of the top of the pineapple. Slice about 1 inch off the bottom. Stand the pineapple up and slice off the skin, cutting down from top to bottom and working your way around. Remove the "eyes" by cutting out grooves, following the diagonal lines of the eyes.

Holding the trimmed pineapple firmly, cut it into slices. Cut out the center core from the middle of each slice with a paring knife or a sharp round cutter.

CHERRY COMPOTE WITH BALSAMIC VINEGAR

This is adapted from Lindsey Shere's Chez Panisse Desserts, *one of my favorite books. Shere says, "When Alice [Waters] was trying to cook some underripe cherries early in the season, she discovered that balsamic vinegar magically brings out their flavor." They added a bit of kirsch; I prefer the compote without.*

serves 4

1 pound ripe Bing cherries, pitted
2 tablespoons light brown sugar
2 teaspoons balsamic vinegar
1 to 2 pints vanilla gelato or ice cream

1. Put the cherries in a large skillet, sprinkle with the sugar, and cook over medium-high heat for about 5 minutes, or until the sugar is dissolved and the cherries are softened. Sprinkle the vinegar over the cherries and cook, stirring, for 1 minute. Serve warm, or let cool to room temperature, then refrigerate, tightly covered, for up to 3 days.

2. To serve, scoop the gelato into four serving bowls. Spoon the cherry compote over the top, and serve immediately.

*It's my dream
to eat ice cream
and keep my shirt clean,
and it's known
that a cone
is safer
than a wafer.*

*

—NORMAN HOLLANDS

DRIED PEACH, APRICOT, AND CHERRY COMPOTE

A classic wintertime fruit compote. I think it's best served warm. If you have some of the compote left over, it keeps well in the refrigerator.

serves 4

1 cup apple cider or apple juice

½ cup dried peaches, each cut into 3 strips

½ cup dried apricots, each cut into 3 strips

2 tablespoons light brown sugar

2 strips lemon zest removed with a
   vegetable peeler

½ cinnamon stick

¼ cup dried sour cherries

¼ teaspoon pure vanilla extract

1 to 2 pints vanilla ice cream

1. Combine the apple cider, peaches, apricots, sugar, zest, and cinnamon stick in a medium saucepan and bring to a boil over high heat. Reduce the heat to low and simmer for 5 minutes.

2. Transfer the mixture to a bowl and add the cherries and vanilla. Serve warm or at room temperature, or let cool and refrigerate, tightly covered, for up to 3 weeks.

3. To serve, scoop the ice cream into four serving bowls or glasses. Spoon the fruit compote over the ice cream, drizzle with some of the syrup remaining in the bowl, and serve immediately.

POACHED APRICOTS

When cooked this way, even underripe apricots are delicious. If you'd like, add a few blueberries for garnish—apricots and blueberries taste very good together and look terrific.

serves 4

8 large apricots, halved and pitted, pits reserved
⅔ cup sugar
¾ teaspoon finely grated lemon zest
3 tablespoons fresh lemon juice
⅛ teaspoon pure vanilla extract
1 to 2 pints vanilla ice cream

1. Bring 1 cup water, the apricot pits, sugar, lemon zest, and juice to a boil in a medium saucepan over high heat. Reduce the heat to low and simmer, covered, for 10 minutes.

2. Pour the syrup through a strainer set over a bowl. Wash the saucepan, return the syrup to the pan, add the apricots, and bring to a boil. Reduce the heat to low and simmer about 2 minutes, or just until the apricots begin to soften (they will continue to cook in the syrup). Stir in the vanilla. Serve immediately, or let cool to room temperature and refrigerate, tightly covered, for up to 3 days.

3. To serve, place the apricots in four bowls. Add scoops of the ice cream, drizzle with the syrup remaining in the saucepan, and serve immediately.

mangoes with lime

Simply elegant.

1 tablespoon fresh lime juice

1 tablespoon honey

1 teaspoon finely grated lime zest

2 ripe mangoes, peeled and sliced

1 to 2 pints vanilla ice cream

1. Stir together the lime juice, honey, and lime zest in a small bowl.

2. To serve, arrange the mango slices on four dessert plates. Place scoops of the ice cream to the side, drizzle with the honey mixture, and serve immediately.

how to cut up a mango

Holding the mango firmly on a cutting board, cut off the flesh in a single slice along one side of the flat seed. Repeat on the other side of the mango. For mango cubes, turn each mango half skin side down, and deeply score the flesh lengthwise, then crosswise, being careful not to cut through to the peel. Bend the skin inside out, then slice along it to remove the cubed fruit. Or, for slices, cut the flesh lengthwise only, then cut off the slices.

warm mango and basil compote

Adapted from a recipe of Ken Hom's in Good Food Magazine. *Don't shred the basil leaves until the last minute, or they will darken.*

serves 6

⅓ cup sugar
3 large ripe mangoes, peeled and sliced
½ cup ripe raspberries
¼ teaspoon pure vanilla extract
Pinch of salt
6 small fresh basil leaves, finely shredded
2 tablespoons unsalted butter
2 pints vanilla ice cream

1. Combine ½ cup water and the sugar in a large skillet over medium heat and heat, stirring, until the sugar is dissolved. Add the mango slices, raspberries, vanilla, and salt and bring to a simmer. Simmer for 2 minutes, or just until heated through. Remove the pan from the heat and stir in the basil and butter.

2. To serve, place scoops of the ice cream in six serving bowls. Top with the mangoes, drizzle with the syrup remaining in the pan, and serve immediately.

chocolate-covered Bananas

Frozen chocolate-coated bananas on a stick were my favorite childhood beach snack in Santa Cruz, California. Immediately after coating them with chocolate, you can roll the bananas in toasted coconut or chopped salted peanuts—about one cup of either, spread on a piece of wax paper, would be just right. The bananas are wonderful served with scoops of ice cream and would push a banana split right over the edge of over-the-top. (Don't forget to pull off all those strings on the bananas.)

makes 4 bananas

One 6-ounce package (1 cup) semisweet chocolate chips, or 6 ounces bittersweet or semisweet chocolate, finely chopped
4 teaspoons unsalted butter or flavorless vegetable oil
4 large bananas, peeled
1 to 2 pints vanilla ice cream
Warm or Cool Chocolate Sauce (page 175), optional

1. Place a large plate lined with wax paper in the freezer for 10 minutes.

2. Melt the chocolate with the butter in a heatproof bowl set over a saucepan of simmering water, stirring until smooth. Pour the chocolate mixture into a glass pie plate.

3. Roll each banana in the chocolate, spooning chocolate over any hard-to-reach spots, shake off any excess, and place on the wax-paper-lined plate. Freeze for at least 30 minutes, or until the chocolate is set; or for 2 hours, until the bananas are frozen.

4. To serve, place the bananas on four chilled plates. Add scoops of the ice cream, drizzle with the chocolate sauce, if using, and serve immediately.

warm FIGS WITH PINe nuts

Is there anyone who doesn't love fresh figs? They are delightful just the way they are, but prepared this way, they're perfect. With vanilla ice cream, they make a luscious, simple dessert.

serves 4

2 tablespoons unsalted butter
2 tablespoons light brown sugar
6 ripe figs, stemmed and halved
⅛ teaspoon pure vanilla extract
1 to 2 pints vanilla ice cream
2 tablespoons toasted pine nuts

1. Melt the butter in a large nonstick skillet over medium heat. Add the sugar and cook, stirring, until it has partially melted. Add the figs and vanilla and cook, gently turning the figs once, for about 4 minutes, or until they are softened.

2. To serve, scoop the ice cream into four serving bowls or glasses. Spoon the figs over the ice cream, drizzle with some of the syrup remaining in the pan, and top with the pine nuts. Serve immediately.

HONEY-AND-THYME-POACHED FIGS

This has terrific Mediterranean-style taste, and its sunny flavors are available even in the dead of winter.

serves 4

1 cup dry white wine

½ cup white grape juice

1 tablespoon honey

½ teaspoon fresh thyme leaves

¼ teaspoon pure vanilla extract

8 ounces dried Calimyrna figs, stemmed, halved, and each half cut into 5 thin strips

1 tablespoon thin julienne strips lemon zest

1 to 2 pints vanilla ice cream

1. Combine the wine, grape juice, honey, thyme, and vanilla in a medium saucepan and bring to a boil over medium-high heat. Add the figs and lemon zest, reduce the heat to low, and simmer, partially covered, for 5 minutes, or until the figs are softened.

2. To serve, scoop the ice cream into four serving bowls or glasses. Spoon the figs over the ice cream, drizzle with the syrup remaining in the saucepan, and serve immediately.

oranges and dates

You might add to the Middle Eastern flavors of this lovely, simple dish by sprinkling it with finely ground bright green pistachios. Orange-flower water is available in many supermarkets, specialty food stores, and Middle Eastern markets.

serves 4

2 oranges, peeled with a sharp knife, thinly sliced crosswise, and seeded
1 tablespoon confectioners' sugar
½ teaspoon orange-flower water, optional
6 pitted dates, thinly sliced crosswise
1 pint vanilla ice cream

Arrange the oranges on four small plates or in shallow serving bowls. Sprinkle with the sugar and orange-flower water, if using, and top with the dates. Place scoops of the ice cream over or next to the oranges, and serve immediately.

Baked Rhubarb with Raspberries

Rhubarb is most pleasant if it retains its shape when served, and baking it is the best way I know to make sure it doesn't get mushy. Feel free to add minced crystallized ginger before cooking, or a tiny bit of rose water after cooking.

serves 4

½ pint fresh raspberries

¾ cup packed light brown sugar

1 pound rhubarb, trimmed and cut into
    ½-inch-thick slices (about 4 cups)

2 tablespoons unsalted butter, cut into
    small pieces

¼ teaspoon pure vanilla extract

Pinch of salt

1 to 2 pints vanilla ice cream

1. Preheat the oven to 350 degrees F.

2. Puree the raspberries with the sugar and ¼ cup boiling water in a food processor. Pour the mixture through a strainer set over a bowl, pressing hard on the solids to extract as much liquid as possible. Stir in the rhubarb, butter, vanilla, and salt.

3. Transfer the mixture to a 7 × 11-inch glass baking dish. Bake for 30 minutes, or until softened, stirring very gently halfway through. Let cool for 10 minutes.

4. To serve, scoop the ice cream into four serving bowls or glasses. Spoon the fruit mixture over the ice cream, drizzle with the syrup remaining in the baking dish, and serve immediately.

clementines with cardamom

If you'd like, add a tablespoon or so of orange liqueur to the syrup. If you don't have green cardamom pods, you can use white ones, but the green look especially good with the clementines.

serves 4

¼ **cup sugar**

1 **cinnamon stick**

2 **strips lemon zest removed with a vegetable peeler**

3 **green cardamom pods, crushed**

4 **clementines, peeled, halved crosswise, and seeded**

1 **to 2 pints vanilla ice cream**

Finely chopped pistachios, optional

1. Combine ¾ cup water, the sugar, cinnamon stick, zest, and cardamom in a medium saucepan and bring to a boil over high heat, stirring until the sugar is dissolved. Boil for 5 minutes.

2. Arrange the clementine halves, cut side up, in an 8-inch square glass dish. Pour the hot syrup over the clementines and let cool to room temperature. Serve immediately, or let stand at room temperature for up to 2 hours.

3. To serve, arrange 2 clementine halves in each of four bowls. Place scoops of the ice cream next to the clementines, sprinkle with the pistachios, if using, and serve immediately.

caramel apples

Why should shortcakes be just for summertime? For a winter shortcake, serve these apples with Shortcakes (page 137) or as is.

serves 6

¾ cup heavy cream

⅓ cup plus 1 tablespoon sugar

2 tablespoons light corn syrup

Pinch of salt

4 tablespoons (½ stick) unsalted butter

5 Granny Smith apples (about 2 pounds), peeled, cored, and cut into 8 wedges each

1 to 2 pints vanilla ice cream

1. Heat the cream in a small saucepan over medium heat just until hot. Set aside, covered, to keep warm.

2. Heat ⅓ cup of the sugar and the corn syrup in a small heavy saucepan over medium heat, stirring until the sugar is dissolved. Increase the heat to high and bring to a boil, washing down the sides of the pan with a damp pastry brush if you see any sugar crystals on the sides. Boil, without stirring, until the caramel turns a dark golden brown, continuing to wash down the sides of the pan with the pastry brush if necessary. Immediately remove the pan from the heat and, being careful to avoid spatters, add the cream about 2 tablespoons at a time, stirring gently. Return the pan to low heat and whisk until the sauce is smooth. Add the salt, and remove from the heat.

3. Melt the butter in a large heavy skillet over medium-high heat. Add the apples and cook, stirring gently, until lightly browned. Add the remaining 1 tablespoon sugar and cook until the apples are soft and caramelized. Add the caramel sauce and stir gently.

4. To serve, scoop the ice cream into six serving bowls or glasses. Spoon the fruit mixture over the ice cream, drizzle with some of the caramel syrup, and serve immediately.

Drizzle sliced sugared strawberries with passion fruit juice and serve over orange ice cream and/or sorbet, topped with Passion Fruit Whipped Cream (page 209)

Toss strawberries with sugar, Armagnac, and a pinch of black pepper, for Strawberries Carcassonne, and serve with vanilla ice cream; or toss whole strawberries (or halved and pitted apricots) with sifted confectioners' sugar, coating well, thread on skewers, and grill until just beginning to brown and caramelize, and serve with ice cream

Spoon Roasted Strawberries (page 146) over strawberry cheesecake ice cream

Stir together fresh blackberries with a little sugar, a splash of Beaumes-de-Venise or other dessert wine, and a pinch of grated lemon zest, and let stand just until some of the juices are released; use as a topping for vanilla gelato

Serve fresh raspberries and pitted fresh Queen Anne cherries with raspberry ice cream, or serve fresh raspberries and fresh or canned lychees over raspberry sorbet

Stir raspberries and sugar together and let stand until they form a sauce; spoon over quartered ripe black and green figs, alongside raspberry sorbet

Gently cook raspberries and blackberries in a bit of butter and sugar, add a splash of orange liqueur and a pinch of orange zest, and serve with vanilla raspberry swirl ice cream

Combine mixed summer berries with sugar and a few crushed unsprayed scented geranium leaves, and refrigerate, tightly covered, for at least 2 and up to 4 hours; discard the geranium leaves before serving with vanilla and/or berry ice cream

Toss sugared blueberries with diced mangoes and serve with mango sorbet, or drizzle raspberry sorbet and vanilla ice cream with crème de cassis and top with fresh blueberries

Stir blueberries into warm Old-fashioned Caramel Sauce (page 181) and spoon over vanilla gelato

Stir together sliced peaches, brown sugar, a drop of balsamic vinegar, and a pinch of cracked black pepper and serve over peach or vanilla ice cream

Toss sliced white peaches and golden raspberries with a drop or two of rose water and serve over peach ice cream

Top sliced white peaches and/or nectarines with Blackberry Sauce (page 187) and serve with peach or raspberry frozen yogurt

Slice ripe yellow or white peaches and toss with a bit of sugar and a large pinch of finely grated lemon zest for a great shortcake topping; especially good with ginger, strawberry, or vanilla ice cream

Lightly sprinkle ripe peeled peach halves with sugar, brush with butter, and grill, cut side down, until slightly softened and browned, and serve with Raspberry Sauce (page 187) and vanilla raspberry swirl ice cream; or grill ripe peach halves, top each with crumbled amaretti, and serve with caramel ice cream or gelato

Gently poach halved peeled white peaches in white dessert wine with a pinch of lemon zest, and serve on vanilla ice cream; or macerate canned peach halves in dessert wine with lemon zest and vanilla, and serve over vanilla and/or lemon ice cream

Arrange canned peach halves in a shallow baking dish, fill the hollows with syrup from jarred preserved ginger, and bake at 350 degrees F until they begin to brown, then sprinkle with a little minced preserved ginger and serve with ginger gelato or ice cream

Stir together pomegranate seeds and sugared sliced ripe nectarines for a gorgeous garnish, and serve with pistachio ice cream

Slice ripe apricots and strawberries, toss with orange juice, and let stand for about 10 minutes; serve as a topping for vanilla ice cream, with a drizzle of Old-fashioned Caramel Sauce (page 181), Caramel Syrup (page 199), or store-bought caramel sauce, and a sprinkling of chopped pistachios

Arrange pitted apricots in a shallow baking dish, sprinkle with sugar and a dash of amaretto, and bake at 350 degrees F until heated through; serve with pralines and cream or vanilla ice cream

Cook sliced dried apricots in a little water with sugar and cardamom for a couple of minutes, just until they are softened; let cool slightly and serve over pistachio ice cream

Drizzle sliced pears with crème de cassis and serve next to blueberry gelato or ice cream

Lightly sprinkle cantaloupe or mixed melon balls or chunks with a combination of ground allspice
berries and white, pink, and black peppercorns; serve over vanilla gelato and/or lime sorbet

Stir together melon balls or cubes with Midori and minced crystallized ginger, and serve with
ginger ice cream

Serve small scoops of assorted sorbets over thin ribbons of honeydew melon and cantaloupe

Make kebabs with cubes of mango, papaya, and banana, brush with a mixture of honey, lime zest,
and juice, and a bit of melted butter, and broil or grill; serve with lime and/or coconut sorbet

Marinate pitted ripe cherries in port or brandy for several hours, then spoon over cinnamon or vanilla
ice cream, or a combination; or heat homemade or store-bought chocolate sauce, stir in pitted
ripe cherries, and serve over cherry vanilla or cherry chocolate ice cream

Top pistachio ice cream with amarena cherries (see page 196) and sprinkle with chopped pistachios
and/or candied orange peel

Toss halved seedless red or black grapes with honey and fresh thyme or mint, and serve on margarita
sorbet

Peel and seed ripe red papayas, cut into long thin slices, and arrange on chilled plates; drizzle with
fresh lime juice, and serve with lime sorbet, or with lime sorbet and vanilla ice cream

Sprinkle cubes of fresh pineapple with toasted shaved coconut and serve with coconut sorbet and/or
gelato

Cut very ripe passion fruits (those with withered skin) in half and spoon out the flesh onto mango
sorbet or coconut sorbet or gelato

Top mango slices with coconut gelato and drizzle with Smooth Strawberry Sauce (page 188)

Grill halved and peeled mangoes and serve with coconut gelato, topped with toasted coconut or
crushed Praline (page xxxix)

Drizzle halved ripe Black Mission figs with lavender honey and serve with honey or caramel gelato; or
gently stir halved ripe figs with honey and orange-flower water and serve over orange ice cream

Make a syrup of honey, port, and a squeeze of lemon juice, then steep stemmed dried figs in the
warm syrup, with a bit of vanilla, overnight at room temperature, and serve over caramel or

cinnamon ice cream; or steep sliced dried green figs in hazelnut liqueur and serve over chocolate ice cream

Serve Baked Rhubarb with Raspberries (page 161) with pistachio ice cream, perhaps on Toasted Brioche (page 142)

Drizzle sliced oranges with Caramel Syrup (page 199) or Grand Marnier and serve with orange sorbet and vanilla ice cream, or with caramel ice cream or gelato

Serve sliced blood oranges, sprinkled with a pinch of freshly grated nutmeg and drizzled with orange liqueur, next to vanilla ice cream and blood orange sorbet

Top thinly sliced oranges or tangerines with tiny ripe strawberries tossed with orange-flower water and sugar; serve over orange and cream ice cream

Drizzle blood orange and tangerine segments with orange liqueur, sprinkle with the tiniest pinch of ground cardamom, and serve over vanilla ice cream and orange sorbet

Macerate sliced oranges in marmalade and orange liqueur and serve over chocolate gelato or ice cream

Toss sliced kumquats with orange liqueur and serve over vanilla ice cream and orange sorbet

Top grilled or broiled bananas with banana ice cream, Passion Fruit Caramel Sauce (page 182), and chopped macadamia nuts, or top with vanilla ice cream, chocolate sauce, and hazelnuts

Stir together chopped dates, dried figs, and sliced dried apricots with maple syrup and spoon over maple walnut ice cream

Age does not diminish the extreme disappointment
of having a scoop of ice cream fall from the cone.

✳

—JIM FIEBIG

8

SAUCY SAUCES AND TOPPINGS, FLAVORED SYRUPS, AND SLIGHTLY SWEETENED WHIPPED CREAMS

Sauces are where all the fun begins. A bowl of ice cream with hot fudge or raspberry sauce is a good-time celebration. Bring it to the table, and eyes begin to sparkle.

There is a full range of sauces here, beginning, of course, with chocolate—nine different chocolate sauces alone. If you venture past the chocolate, you'll find caramel, coffee, marshmallow, fruit and berry sauces, a couple of nut and dried fruit toppings, and a sauce to get you out of any dessert jam.

Ultrapasteurized cream may not be your favorite for whipping, but it comes in handy for making sauces. The sauces will last as long as the cream, which is a good long time, up to 2 months.

Several of the fruit and berry sauces and toppings are made with confectioners' sugar, which contains a small amount of cornstarch and very slightly thickens the juices of the fruits, without making them too thick or gloppy.

If you store the sauces in jars, you can heat any of them in the jar, lid removed, in a saucepan of simmering water, then just stir (or cover with the lid and shake) before serving.

Flavored syrups are versatile and great to have on hand, making it possible for you to whip up desserts on a whim. Use them for fountain drinks, especially sodas, or drinks with alcohol, or as toppings for coupes, sundaes, parfaits, or splits. Toss them with cut fresh fruits or berries for almost instant ice cream toppings; use as a drizzle for ice-cream-filled pies, cakes, and meringues; or serve as sauces for terrines, bonbons, or bombes. Or use for flavoring whipped creams.

They take just a few minutes to make and keep very well in the refrigerator, many of them for months. Refrigerate them, tightly covered, in glass jars and shake them very well before serving them chilled. (Shaking is much easier and more efficient than transferring them into a bowl and whisking them.)

easiest HOT FUDGe sauce

Heat some cream and corn syrup, throw in chocolate, and whisk until smooth—I don't want to keep you from your ice cream for too long.

makes 1½ cups

1 cup heavy cream
2 tablespoons light corn syrup
8 ounces bittersweet or semisweet chocolate,
    finely chopped

1. Bring the cream and corn syrup just to a boil in a large saucepan over medium-high heat. Remove the pan from the heat, add the chocolate, and whisk until smooth.

2. Use immediately, or let cool to room temperature, transfer to a glass jar, and refrigerate, tightly covered, for up to 2 months. Gently reheat before serving.

To resist is hopeless. Your existence is meaningless without ice cream.

*

—ice cream Truck in the TV show
INVADER ZIM

OLD-Fashioned Hot Fudge sauce

If you want a sauce that hardens and becomes chewy when it hits cold ice cream, this is it. Use a heavy saucepan, and you won't have to worry about the sauce burning.

MAKES 1½ CUPS

1 cup heavy cream
3 ounces bittersweet or semisweet chocolate,
    finely chopped
2 tablespoons unsalted butter
2 tablespoons light corn syrup
½ cup packed dark brown sugar
1 teaspoon pure vanilla extract
Pinch of salt

1. Heat the cream, chocolate, butter, and corn syrup in a large heavy saucepan over medium-low heat, whisking, until the chocolate is melted. Add the sugar and whisk until dissolved. Increase the heat to medium-high, bring to a boil, and boil, whisking occasionally, for 6 minutes, until the mixture is slightly thickened.

2. Immediately transfer the sauce to a glass measure or heatproof bowl. Stir in the vanilla and salt. Use immediately, or let cool to room temperature, transfer to a glass jar, and refrigerate, tightly covered, for up to 2 months. Gently reheat before serving.

warm or cool chocolate sauce

Having this on hand all but guarantees a better life. It's magic drizzled on ice-cream-filled profiteroles, meringues piled high with ice cream, sorbet, and fruit, or angel food cake and strawberries, or simply lavished on scoops of coffee gelato. I'm not sure I can think of any dessert it wouldn't be good with.

MAKES 2 CUPS

One 12-ounce package (2 cups) semisweet chocolate chips or 12 ounces bittersweet or semisweet chocolate, finely chopped
½ cup heavy cream
Pinch of salt

1. Melt the chocolate with the cream, 6 tablespoons water, and the salt in a heatproof bowl set over a saucepan of simmering water, whisking until smooth.

2. Use immediately, or let cool to room temperature, transfer to a glass jar, and refrigerate, tightly covered, for up to 2 months. Shake well before serving chilled, or gently reheat before serving.

VARIATIONS

Add a teaspoon or so of instant espresso powder along with the salt.

Add crushed peppermint candies after the sauce cools slightly.

Stir in a large pinch of orange or lemon zest and let stand for 5 to 10 minutes; strain if you want to.

Add a couple of tablespoons or so of your favorite liqueur or spirit once cooled.

Stir in about ¼ cup toasted chopped nuts or shredded coconut.

Stir in a handful of pitted fresh, canned, or dried sour cherries. Or try golden raisins or dried strawberries.

Flavor the sauce with jam, preserves, or marmalade; strain if desired.

LIGHTer CHOCOLATE sauce

No cream, no butter, just deep dark chocolate. Feel free to substitute a tablespoon or so of your favorite liqueur or spirit for the same amount of water.

MAKES 2 CUPS

8 ounces bittersweet or semisweet chocolate,
    finely chopped
¾ to 1 cup water or brewed coffee
Pinch of salt

1. Melt the chocolate with the water and salt in a heatproof bowl set over a saucepan of simmering water, whisking until smooth.

2. Use immediately, or let cool to room temperature, transfer to a glass jar, and refrigerate, tightly covered, for up to 3 months. Shake well before serving chilled, or gently reheat before serving.

serious CHOCOLATE sauce

This is my favorite chocolate sauce—I think of it as "Black Satin." If only it were right in there with fresh fruits and vegetables on the food pyramid! It may not be, but it is definitely good for the soul.

MAKES 1¾ CUPS

One 8-ounce container crème fraîche
8 ounces bittersweet or semisweet chocolate,
    finely chopped

1. Heat the crème fraîche in a heavy medium saucepan over the lowest heat just until liquid. Add the chocolate and whisk until smooth.

2. Use immediately, or let cool to room temperature, transfer to a glass jar, and refrigerate, tightly covered, for up to 2 months. Gently reheat before serving.

chocolate raspberry sauce

Use any other berry or fruit of your choice, cut into small pieces. I especially like chocolate sauce with a layer of peach, cherry, or apricot flavor.

makes 1½ cups

1 cup heavy cream

¾ cup fresh raspberries or thawed frozen raspberries

4 ounces bittersweet or semisweet chocolate, finely chopped

1. Heat the cream, raspberries, and chocolate in a medium heavy saucepan over low heat, stirring until the chocolate is melted. Pour the sauce through a large fine strainer set over a bowl, pressing hard on the solids to extract as much liquid as possible.

2. Use immediately, or let cool to room temperature, transfer to a glass jar, and refrigerate, tightly covered, for up to 2 weeks. Shake well before serving chilled, or gently reheat before serving.

chocolate marshmallow sauce

You might think this would be total kid stuff, but it's not. It has an unusual, very pleasant texture. I think of it as quite sophisticated, like an Italian meringue flavored with fine chocolate. You could make it with milk chocolate for serving to children.

MAKES ABOUT 2 CUPS

4 ounces bittersweet or semisweet chocolate,
    finely chopped
1 cup marshmallow cream

1. Heat the chocolate and ⅔ cup water in a medium saucepan over low heat, whisking until smooth. Remove the pan from the heat and whisk in the marshmallow cream, in three additions, until smooth.

2. Use immediately, or let cool to room temperature, transfer to a glass jar, and refrigerate, tightly covered, for up to 2 months. Gently reheat before serving, adding a little water, if necessary, to thin the sauce slightly.

milk chocolate–peanut butter sauce

If you want a simply lovely milk chocolate sauce without peanut butter, just leave it out. This just may be the perfect topping for a brownie sundae. It's best not to use old-fashioned-style or freshly ground peanut butter for this, or the sauce may separate; use the supermarket variety.

makes 1½ cups

1 cup heavy cream
¼ cup smooth or chunky peanut butter
One 6-ounce package (1 cup) milk chocolate
    chips, or 6 ounces milk chocolate, finely
    chopped

1. Bring the cream and peanut butter just to a boil in a medium saucepan over medium heat, whisking until smooth. Reduce the heat to low, add the chocolate, and whisk until smooth.
2. Use immediately, or let cool to room temperature, transfer to a glass jar, and refrigerate, tightly covered, for up to 2 months. Gently reheat before serving, adding a little water, if necessary, to thin the sauce slightly.

white chocolate sauce

Pool the sauce on a plate and serve with sorbet and fruits or contrasting colors of sorbet, like orange and chocolate. If you want to add the liqueur, use a clear one, so it doesn't turn the sauce an unappealing beige.

MAKES ABOUT 2 CUPS

1 cup heavy cream
2 strips lemon zest removed with a vegetable
      peeler
Pinch of salt
One 11-ounce bag white chocolate chips
2 tablespoons orange liqueur or other liqueur,
      optional

1. Bring the cream, zest, and salt to a boil in a medium saucepan over medium-high heat. Reduce the heat to low, add the white chocolate chips, and whisk until smooth. Add the liqueur, if using. Remove and discard the lemon zest.

2. Use immediately, or let cool to room temperature, transfer to a glass jar, and refrigerate, tightly covered, for up to 2 months. Shake well before serving chilled, or gently reheat before serving.

OLD-FASHIONED caramel sauce

Don't use a saucepan with a dark interior, or it'll be too difficult to judge the color of the caramel. You need to follow the directions faithfully when making caramel, but there is great flexibility in flavoring the sauce after it's made; following the recipe are some suggestions.

MAKES 2 CUPS

1 cup heavy cream
2 cups sugar
2 tablespoons light corn syrup
Pinch of salt

1. Heat the cream in a small saucepan over medium heat just until hot. Set aside, covered, to keep warm.

2. Combine the sugar, ¾ cup water, and the corn syrup in a large heavy saucepan and heat over medium heat, stirring, until the sugar is dissolved. Increase the heat to high and bring to a boil, washing down the sides of the pan with a damp pastry brush if you see any sugar crystals on the sides. Boil, without stirring, until the caramel turns a dark golden brown, continuing to wash down the sides of the pan with the pastry brush if necessary.

3. Immediately remove the saucepan from the heat and, being careful to avoid spatters, whisk in the cream about 2 tablespoons at a time. Return the pan to low heat and heat, whisking, until the sauce is smooth. Remove from the heat and whisk in the salt. Strain the sauce, if desired.

4. Use immediately, or let cool to room temperature, transfer to a glass jar, and refrigerate, tightly covered, for up to 2 months. Gently reheat the sauce before serving, adding a little water or cream, if necessary, to thin the sauce slightly.

variations

Chocolate: Melt 4 ounces bittersweet, semisweet, or milk chocolate, finely chopped, with 3 tablespoons warm water. Whisk into the sauce after stirring in the cream.

Buttery caramel: For an even richer sauce, stir in 2 to 3 tablespoons unsalted butter, cut into small pieces, after adding the cream.

Pine nut, hazelnut, walnut, pecan, peanut, or almond: Stir in ½ to 1 cup toasted whole or chopped nuts after stirring in the cream.

Coffee: Dissolve a teaspoon or two of instant espresso powder in the warm cream.

Citrus: Flavor the cream with grated zest and fresh juice to taste, or a tiny bit of one of Boyajian's pure citrus oils, available at specialty food stores.

Boiled apple cider jelly: Stir in 3 to 4 tablespoons of the jelly after adding the cream.

Liqueur or spirit: Add 2 to 4 tablespoons of your favorite liqueur or spirit to the finished sauce.

Ginger: Add ¼ cup minced crystallized ginger to the hot cream and let steep for 10 minutes. Strain the sauce or not, depending on your preference.

Saffron (or spice): Steep a pinch of crumbled saffron threads or another spice in the hot cream—try cardamom, cinnamon, nutmeg, or allspice.

Rosemary: Steep a small sprig of fresh rosemary in the cream for 10 minutes, then strain. Basil, thyme, and lemon verbena are also terrific.

Peanut butter: Whisk in ¼ cup smooth peanut butter after stirring in the cream.

Fruits and berries: Whisk up to ¾ cup thick fruit syrup or pureed fruit, such as passion fruit or bananas, into the finished sauce.

SCOTTISH-STYLE BUTTERSCOTCH SAUCE

Butterscotch candy originated in Scotland, and we Americans turned it into a sauce for use over ice cream, cake, and other sweets. This sauce has the true taste of the Scottish candy.

MAKES 1½ CUPS

4 tablespoons (½ stick) unsalted butter
¾ cup packed dark brown sugar
1 cup heavy cream
Pinch of salt

1. Melt the butter in a heavy medium saucepan over medium heat. Add the sugar and heat, whisking, until dissolved. Add the cream and salt, increase the heat to high, and bring to a boil. Boil for 5 minutes.

2. Use immediately, or let cool to room temperature, transfer to a glass jar, and refrigerate, tightly covered, for up to 2 months. Gently reheat before serving.

HOT BUTTERED RUM SAUCE

Also try spiced rum or coconut rum here. Actually, you don't need to use rum at all— this could be hot buttered just about anything, from Cognac or another brandy to bourbon.

MAKES 1½ CUPS

8 tablespoons (1 stick) unsalted butter
1 cup packed dark brown sugar
½ cup heavy cream
2 tablespoons dark rum

1. Melt the butter in a medium saucepan over medium heat. Add the sugar and heat, whisking, until dissolved. Add the cream, increase the heat to high, and bring to a boil. Boil for 4 minutes, or until the sauce is reduced to about 1½ cups. Remove the pan from the heat and, when the sauce stops bubbling, whisk in the rum.
2. Use immediately, or let cool to room temperature, transfer to a glass jar, and refrigerate, tightly covered, for up to 2 months. Gently reheat before serving.

COFFEE SAUCE

Use espresso if you adore it.

MAKES 1 CUP

1¼ cups sugar
1¼ cups strong brewed coffee
2 tablespoons light corn syrup
Pinch of salt

1. Bring the sugar, coffee, and corn syrup to a boil in a large saucepan over high heat. Boil for about 15 minutes, or until the sauce is thickened and coats the back of a spoon; it will continue to thicken as it stands. Stir in the salt.
2. Use immediately, or let cool to room temperature, transfer to a glass jar, and refrigerate, tightly covered, for up to 1 month. Shake well before serving chilled, or gently reheat before serving.

easiest marshmallow sauce

Marshmallows originally contained the roots of the marshmallow plant—now they're based on egg whites and sugar. Serve this over chocolate ice cream, with or without a tiny drizzle of strawberry syrup. Feel free to replace a tablespoon or so of the water with your favorite liqueur or spirit. You might also add crushed hard peppermint or other candies just before serving.

MAKES 1⅓ CUPS

One 7½-ounce jar marshmallow cream

1. With a rubber spatula, scrape the marshmallow cream into a bowl. Add 3 tablespoons of warm water to the jar, screw on the lid, and shake well. Add the liquid to the bowl and whisk until smooth. Thin the sauce with 1 to 2 tablespoons water if necessary.
2. Use immediately, or transfer to a glass jar and store at room temperature, tightly covered, for up to 3 months. Serve at room temperature.

Blueberry sauce

Blueberry sauce is good with just about any fruit or berry ice cream, gelato, frozen yogurt, or sorbet—and it's superb with a combination of vanilla and caramel.

MAKES 1½ CUPS

1 pint fresh blueberries, picked over
½ to ¾ cup confectioners' sugar (depending on the sweetness of the berries)
1 to 2 teaspoons fresh lemon juice

1. Combine the blueberries, sugar, and 2 tablespoons water in a large saucepan and cook over medium heat, stirring occasionally, for 5 minutes, or until the berries are softened and a sauce is formed. Stir in the lemon juice to taste.
2. Use immediately, or let cool to room temperature, transfer to a glass jar, and refrigerate, tightly covered, for up to 1 month. Shake well before serving chilled, or gently reheat before serving.

Berry and cassis sauce

Blackberries are great in this, and, in fact, so are all berries, but I have a personal preference for bluish berries over reddish ones here. The yield of the sauce will depend on how seedy the berries are; you don't need to strain the sauce at all if you use only blueberries.

makes 1½ cups

1 pint fresh or thawed frozen blackberries, boysenberries, and/or blueberries, picked over
¼ cup confectioners' sugar, or to taste
¼ cup crème de cassis

1. Bring the berries, sugar, and 2 tablespoons water to a boil in a large saucepan over medium-high heat. Reduce the heat to low and simmer for 5 minutes, or until the berries are softened and a sauce is formed. Remove the pan from the heat and stir in the crème de cassis.

2. Pour the sauce through a large coarse strainer set over a bowl, pressing hard on the solids to extract as much liquid as possible. Use immediately, or let cool to room temperature, transfer to a glass jar, and refrigerate, tightly covered, for up to 1 month. Shake well before serving chilled, or gently reheat before serving.

raspberry or blackberry sauce

It's always great to have some of this delicious, versatile sauce on hand.

MAKES ABOUT 2 CUPS

3 cups fresh raspberries or blackberries
½ to ¾ cup confectioners' sugar (depending on
    the sweetness of the berries)
1 to 2 teaspoons fresh lemon juice

1.   Puree the raspberries in a food processor. Sift the sugar over the berries, add 2 tablespoons water, and pulse until smooth. Add the lemon juice to taste.

2.   Pour the sauce through a large coarse strainer set over a bowl, pressing hard on the solids to extract as much liquid as possible. Transfer to a glass jar and refrigerate, tightly covered, for up to 1 month. Shake well before serving the sauce chilled; the sauce will thicken a bit on chilling, so add water as needed to thin it to the desired consistency.

smooth strawberry sauce

Use this as a sauce, drizzle, or syrup—you'll find infinite ways to serve it.

makes 1½ cups

1 pint fresh strawberries, hulled and sliced
⅓ to ½ cup light corn syrup (depending on the
   sweetness of the berries)
1 to 2 teaspoons fresh lemon juice

1. Bring the strawberries, corn syrup, and ¼ cup water to a boil in a large saucepan over medium-high heat, stirring occasionally. Reduce the heat to medium and continue boiling, stirring frequently, for 10 minutes. Stir in the lemon juice to taste.

2. Pour the sauce through a large fine strainer set over a bowl, pressing hard on the solids to extract as much liquid as possible. Use immediately, or let cool to room temperature, transfer to a glass jar, and refrigerate, tightly covered, for up to 2 weeks. Shake well before serving chilled, or gently reheat before serving.

sliced strawberry topping

Serve over bowls of ice cream, or with Shortcakes (page 137) and the ice cream and/or sorbet of your choice.

makes 3 cups

1½ pints fresh strawberries, hulled and sliced
¾ to 1 cup confectioners' sugar (depending on
   the sweetness of the berries)
2 to 3 teaspoons fresh lemon juice

1. Stir together all of the ingredients in a bowl. Let stand for at least 20 minutes, or up to several hours, to allow the berries to release their juices.

2. Serve at room temperature.

rosy plum sauce

This sauce may well be the most beautiful color in existence—its bright and vibrant hue flatters all fruit and berry ice creams.

MAKES ABOUT 2 CUPS

6 large ripe purple or red plums (about 1½ pounds), or a combination, pitted and chopped
¼ to ⅓ cup confectioners' sugar (depending on the sweetness of the plums)
2 to 3 teaspoons fresh lemon juice

1. Combine the plums and sugar in a medium saucepan and cook over medium-low heat, stirring frequently, for 15 minutes, or until the plums are very soft. Let cool slightly, and stir in the lemon juice to taste.

2. Puree the sauce in a food processor. Pour through a large coarse strainer set over a bowl, pressing hard on the solids to extract as much liquid as possible.

3. Use immediately, or let cool to room temperature, transfer to a glass jar, and refrigerate, tightly covered, for up to 3 weeks. Shake well before serving chilled, or gently reheat before serving.

raspberry plum sauce

Take advantage of late-summer plums and the raspberries that ripen at the same time for this sauce.

MAKES ABOUT 2 CUPS

**4 large ripe purple or red plums (about 1 pound),
    or a combination, pitted and chopped**
½ pint fresh raspberries
⅓ cup sugar, or to taste
2 to 3 teaspoons fresh lemon juice

1. Combine the plums, raspberries, and sugar in a medium saucepan and cook over low heat, stirring frequently, for about 15 minutes, or until the plums are very soft; add 1 to 2 tablespoons water if the mixture seems dry. Stir in the lemon juice to taste.

2. Pour the sauce through a large coarse strainer set over a bowl, pressing hard on the solids to extract as much liquid as possible. Use immediately, or let cool to room temperature, transfer to a glass jar, and refrigerate, tightly covered, for up to 3 weeks. Shake well before serving chilled, or gently reheat before serving.

how much fruit to buy

A 1-pint container of strawberries equals about 3½ cups whole berries or 2¼ cups sliced.

A ½-pint container of raspberries or blackberries equals 1 cup.

One pound peaches or nectarines (3 medium) equals 2¼ cups peeled and sliced, or 2 cups peeled and diced.

One pound plums (4 or 5 medium) equals 3 cups sliced or diced.

One pound cherries equals about 3 cups whole or 2 cups pitted.

One pound apricots (6 medium) equals 1 cup sliced.

One pound grapes equals 3 cups stemmed.

cherry sauce

Serve with crème fraîche sorbet or just about anything chocolate. Use vegetable oil rather than butter if you want to serve the sauce chilled or at room temperature.

MAKES ABOUT 1½ CUPS

1 tablespoon unsalted butter or flavorless
   vegetable oil
12 ounces (2 cups) ripe Bing cherries, pitted
2 to 3 tablespoons light brown sugar

1.   Melt the butter in a medium nonstick skillet over medium heat. Add the cherries and cook, stirring frequently, for 3 to 5 minutes, until they begin to release their juices. Add the sugar to taste, increase the heat to high, and bring to a boil. Reduce the heat to low and simmer, stirring, for 4 minutes, or until the sugar has dissolved and the juices have thickened slightly. Remove the skillet from the heat and let cool slightly.

2.   Use immediately, or let cool to room temperature, transfer to a jar, and refrigerate, tightly covered, for up to 2 days. Serve chilled or at room temperature, or reheat gently before serving.

dried sour cherry sauce

Dried sour cherries are one of my favorite things. You might also use a lovely combination of golden raisins and dried sour cherries packed by Sunsweet, available in most supermarkets.

MAKES 2½ CUPS

1 cup sugar
8 ounces (1¾ cups) dried sour cherries
3 to 4 tablespoons fresh lemon juice
Pinch of salt

1.   Bring 2½ cups water and the sugar to a boil in a large saucepan over medium-high heat, stirring until the sugar is dissolved. Boil for 5 minutes.

2.   Reduce the heat to low, add the cherries, and simmer, stirring occasionally, for about 12 minutes, or until the cherries are plump and soft. Stir in the lemon juice to taste and add the salt.

3.   Use immediately, or let cool to room temperature, transfer to a glass jar, and refrigerate, tightly covered, for up to 3 months. Serve chilled, or gently reheat before serving.

kumquat sauce with star anise

Spoon over a bowl of vanilla ice cream, and you've got perfect winter comfort.

MAKES 1½ CUPS

½ cup sugar
4 star anise
1 pound kumquats (about 40), thinly sliced
    and seeded
Pinch of salt

1. Bring 1 cup water and the sugar to a boil in a medium saucepan over medium heat, stirring until the sugar is dissolved. Add the star anise and continue to boil for 5 minutes.

2. Stir in the kumquats and salt and simmer for 5 minutes, or until the sauce is slightly thickened. Remove the star anise (reserve for garnish, if desired).

3. Use immediately, or let cool to room temperature, transfer to a glass jar, and refrigerate, tightly covered, for up to 1 week. Serve chilled, or gently reheat before serving.

pineapple sauce

Although pineapple sauce is one of the three traditional sauces on the classic banana split, I often find it a disappointment there. But it really shines served over coconut and/or mango sorbet, gelato, or ice cream.

MAKES 2 CUPS

1 cup sugar
1½ cups finely chopped ripe pineapple
Pinch of salt

1. Bring 1 cup water and the sugar to a boil in a medium saucepan over high heat, stirring until the sugar is dissolved. Boil for 10 minutes.

2. Add the pineapple and salt and boil for 5 minutes longer. Let cool slightly.

3. Use immediately, or let cool to room temperature, transfer to a glass jar, and refrigerate, tightly covered, for up to 2 months. Serve chilled.

persimmon sauce

Of the two basic types of persimmons, Hachiya and Fuyu, I use Hachiya for this sauce, because of their soft texture when ripe. (Fuyu are crunchy even when ripe.) And they must be ripe—if not, they will be very astringent and unpleasant. When fully ripe and ready to use, they are fragrant and as soft as jelly. To ripen firm Hachiya persimmons, place them in a bag with a banana or an apple, close the bag, and let stand at room temperature for 3 to 6 days. This is just the thing served with a square of gingerbread and vanilla ice cream.

MAKES 1½ CUPS

2 large ripe Hachiya persimmons
2 tablespoons fresh lime juice
Pinch of salt

1. Cut the persimmons in half and, with a spoon, scoop the pulp into a food processor. Add the lime juice and salt and process until smooth.

2. Use immediately, or transfer to a glass jar and refrigerate, tightly covered, for up to 2 days. Shake well before serving chilled.

raisins in cognac

You could replace some of the golden raisins with chopped crystallized ginger, or use dried sour cherries instead. Substitute grappa or rum for the Cognac, or add a tiny amount of spice such as star anise, a small piece of a cinnamon stick, an allspice berry, or a few peppercorns. Remove the spices before serving.

MAKES 1½ CUPS

1 cup Cognac or other brandy
¾ cup golden raisins

1. Heat the Cognac and raisins in a small saucepan over medium-low heat just until the raisins are plump and warm; do not boil.

2. Use immediately, or let cool to room temperature, transfer to a glass jar, and store at room temperature, tightly covered, for up to several months.

"in a jam" sauce

Think you've got nothing to put over your ice cream? If you keep a good jar of preserves in the pantry, you'll always be at the ready. I prefer not to puree or strain the sauce—I like it with a little texture. Try Scotch marmalade, ginger preserves, Damson plum jam, sour cherry preserves, or rose petal jam.

MAKES ABOUT 1 CUP

One 12-ounce jar best-quality preserves or
marmalade
2 teaspoons fresh lemon juice
2 to 4 tablespoons water, fruit juice, or liqueur,
or as needed

1. Bring the preserves and lemon juice to a simmer in a medium saucepan over medium heat. Transfer to a food processor and puree. Pour through a fine strainer set over a bowl, if desired. Thin the sauce to the desired consistency with the water.

2. Use immediately, or let cool to room temperature, transfer to a glass jar, and refrigerate, tightly covered, for up to 2 months. Gently reheat before serving.

wet walnuts

This soda fountain classic doesn't have to be made with walnuts—pecans, peanuts, and hazelnuts are also very good. Whichever nuts you use, they should be toasted, to keep them from getting soggy (see page xl). You don't need a lot of this on a dessert; a tablespoon or so might be just enough. Try a spoonful over a hot fudge sundae.

MAKES 1 CUP

1 cup toasted walnut pieces
¼ cup pure maple syrup
¼ cup dark corn syrup

Stir together the walnuts, maple syrup, and corn syrup in a bowl until well combined. Use immediately, or transfer to a glass jar and refrigerate, tightly covered, for up to 2 weeks. Serve chilled or at room temperature.

PINE NUT SAUCE

This is also very good with peeled whole hazelnuts.

MAKES 1½ CUPS

4 tablespoons (½ stick) unsalted butter

1 cup pine nuts

½ cup Caramel Syrup (page 199) or dark corn syrup

1 to 2 tablespoons fresh lemon juice

1. Melt the butter in a medium skillet over medium heat. Add the pine nuts and cook, stirring constantly, until golden brown. Add the syrup and the lemon juice to taste and cook, stirring, for 2 minutes longer.

2. Use immediately, or let cool to room temperature, transfer to a glass jar, and refrigerate, tightly covered, for up to 2 weeks. Gently reheat before serving.

You can use store-bought ingredients to create your own custom sauces.
Here are some ideas to get you started:

- Thin Nutella or other chocolate hazelnut spread with cream, milk, or water and use as a sauce.
- Serve boiled apple cider jelly warm over ice cream (especially good served alongside apple pie).
- Dulce de leche is caramelized cow's milk; cajeta is made with sheep's or goat's milk. Heat either one to use as a sauce.
- Amarena, or amarene, cherries, which come from Vignola, a small town near Modena, Italy, are cherries flavored with almond and preserved in heavy syrup. Fabbri's are the best-known brand; they come in a blue-and-white jar. The same company also makes strawberries in heavy syrup.
- Try warm maple syrup with golden raisins and toasted pecans; you might also add minced crystallized ginger.
- Caramelize 1 cup of honey; heat it until it reaches the darkness you're looking for, then carefully add 6 tablespoons hot water, or thin it to the thickness desired. You can cook a spice or herb with the honey, or add a fruit puree or sauce at the end.
- Minced preserved ginger and its syrup make a great topping as is. Or heat ginger preserves (or marmalade) with a little ginger liqueur.

- Jarred black currant or sour cherry compotes in light syrup, available in Eastern European markets, specialty food stores, and many supermarkets, make terrific toppings.
- Chill some canned mandarin oranges, and just before serving, stir in some fresh raspberries, blueberries, or tiny strawberries.
- Add some fresh lime juice to high-quality canned or jarred sliced mangoes, and use as a topping for ice cream or a garnish for a sundae.
- American Spoon Foods makes a terrific Strawberry Shortcake Sauce. Reach them at www.spoon.com. Maury Island's Red Raspberry Ecstasy Sauce is available from Williams-Sonoma stores or online at www.williams-sonoma.com.
- If a milk chocolate–pecan sauce that hardens immediately on ice cream is just your kind of thing, give Gold Brick sauce a try; available at www.elmercandy.com.

. . . .

mars bar sauce

The secret of generations of bedsitter dwellers, this instant chocolate sauce tastes wonderful over ice creams and puddings. Simply chop two large Mars bars and heat very gently in a small, heavy-based saucepan. When melted, stir well and use at once. For incredible richness, stir in a spoonful or two of thick cream just before serving.

—mary norwak, *MY FAVORITE CHOCOLATE COOKBOOK*

. . . .

ice cream sauce

Pay attention here! This could save you in times of crisis—it makes a fantastic sauce for cakes, brownies, gingerbread, or fruit. It's not for ice cream, it is ice cream. Use your favorite ice cream flavor and add a tablespoon or so of your favorite spirit or liqueur, sauce, or syrup, if you'd like.

MAKES ABOUT 1 CUP

1 cup ice cream, slightly softened

Spoon the ice cream into a food processor and process until smooth and foamy. Serve immediately.

sorbet sauce

As with the Ice Cream Sauce, you could add a tablespoon or so of a spirit or liqueur. I like this best as a sauce for fruit, but I'll bet you can think of many other uses.

MAKES ABOUT 1 CUP

1 cup sorbet, slightly softened

Spoon the sorbet into a food processor and process until smooth. Serve immediately.

CHOCOLATE SYRUP

The combination of cocoa powder and chocolate means lots of chocolate flavor. My favorite cocoa powder is Scharffen Berger natural cocoa, but any type will do. This keeps well, but feel free to halve the recipe.

MAKES 3½ CUPS

½ cup unsweetened cocoa powder
1 cup packed dark brown sugar
¼ cup light corn syrup
4 ounces bittersweet or semisweet chocolate, finely chopped
¼ teaspoon salt
1½ teaspoons pure vanilla extract

1. Whisk together 2 cups water and the cocoa in a large heavy saucepan until almost smooth. Bring to a boil over medium-high heat. Add the sugar, corn syrup, chocolate, and salt and cook, whisking, until the sugar is dissolved. Reduce the heat to low and simmer for 5 minutes. Let cool to room temperature, and whisk in the vanilla.

2. Use immediately, or transfer to a glass jar and refrigerate, tightly covered, for up to 3 months. Shake well before serving chilled, or gently reheat before serving.

caramel syrup

This is one of the most important staples for dessert makers. It has a tremendous number of uses, and it can improve a dish immensely. Rather than adding a single note of sweetness as sugar does, caramel syrup adds bittersweet —more complex, and delicious. Fold this into fresh fruit; drizzle it over sundaes, cakes, pies, or meringue and ice cream desserts; add it to drinks; etc. This makes a big batch, but it lasts for a good long time. If you have a heavy copper pan, this is the time to use it.

MAKES 3 CUPS

3 cups sugar
¼ cup light corn syrup
¼ teaspoon salt

1. Heat 1 cup of water just until warm. Set aside.

2. Heat the sugar, another 1 cup water, and the corn syrup in a large heavy saucepan over medium heat, stirring until the sugar is dissolved. Increase the heat to high and bring to a boil, washing down the sides of the pan with a damp pastry brush if you see any sugar crystals on the sides. Boil, without stirring, until the caramel turns a dark golden brown, continuing to wash down the sides of the pan with the pastry brush if necessary.

3. Immediately remove the saucepan from the heat and, being careful to avoid spatters, whisk in the warm water about 2 tablespoons at a time. Return the pan to low heat and heat, whisking, until the syrup is smooth and thickened. Remove from the heat and whisk in the salt.

4. Use immediately, or let cool, transfer to a glass jar, and store at room temperature, tightly covered, for up to several months. Serve at room temperature, or gently reheat before serving.

coffee syrup

You could use about a tablespoon of instant espresso powder mixed with 1 cup water instead of the brewed coffee. This makes a superb soda with chocolate and/or coffee ice cream or gelato.

MAKES 1½ CUPS

1 cup strong brewed coffee
½ cup packed dark brown sugar
½ cup light corn syrup
Pinch of salt

1. Bring the coffee, sugar, and corn syrup to a boil in a medium saucepan over medium-high heat, stirring until the sugar is dissolved. Continue to boil for 3 minutes. Simmer on low heat until the syrup is smooth and slightly thickened. Remove the pan from the heat and stir in the salt.

2. Use immediately, or let cool to room temperature, transfer to a glass jar, and refrigerate, tightly covered, for up to 2 months. Shake well before serving chilled, or gently reheat before serving.

strawberry syrup

You'll find endless uses for strawberry syrup— drinks, sundaes, parfaits, and banana splits are just the beginning. I especially like it with vanilla ice cream or strawberry sorbet in a chewy meringue, with whipped cream.

MAKES 2½ CUPS

1 pint fresh strawberries, hulled and thinly sliced
½ cup sugar
½ cup light corn syrup
1 tablespoon fresh lemon juice
Pinch of salt

1. Bring the strawberries, 1 cup water, the sugar, and the corn syrup to a boil in a large saucepan over medium-high heat, stirring until the sugar is dissolved. Continue to boil for 10 minutes. Remove from the heat and stir in the lemon juice and salt.

2. Pour the syrup through a large fine strainer set over a bowl, pressing hard on the solids to extract as much liquid as possible. Use immediately, or let cool to room temperature, transfer to a glass jar, and refrigerate, tightly covered, for up to 2 months. Shake well before serving chilled, or gently reheat before serving.

BLUEBERRY SYRUP

Make a big batch of this when blueberries are in season—especially if you can get the wonderful tiny wild blueberries from Maine. Then freeze some of the syrup in self-sealing plastic bags, and you can have a fabulous blueberry ice cream soda, sundae, or whatever occurs to you at any time of the year.

makes 2½ cups

1 pint fresh blueberries, picked over
½ cup sugar
½ cup light corn syrup
1 tablespoon fresh lemon juice
Pinch of salt

1. Bring the berries, 1 cup water, the sugar, and the corn syrup to a boil in a large saucepan over medium-high heat, stirring until the sugar is dissolved. Continue to boil for 10 minutes. Remove from the heat and stir in the lemon juice and salt.

2. Pour the syrup through a large coarse strainer set over a bowl, pressing hard on the solids to extract as much liquid as possible. Use immediately, or let cool to room temperature, transfer to a glass jar, and refrigerate, tightly covered, for up to 2 months. Shake well before serving chilled, or gently reheat before serving.

blackberry, raspberry, and/or boysenberry syrup

This makes a great ice cream soda with a matching or contrasting ice cream flavor.

makes 2½ cups

1 pint fresh blackberries, raspberries,
    or boysenberries, or a combination
½ cup sugar
½ cup light corn syrup
1 tablespoon fresh lemon juice
Pinch of salt

1. Bring the berries, 1 cup water, the sugar, and the corn syrup to a boil in a large saucepan over medium-high heat, stirring until the sugar is dissolved. Continue to boil for 10 minutes. Remove from the heat and stir in the lemon juice and salt.

2. Pour the syrup through a large fine strainer set over a bowl, pressing hard on the solids to extract as much liquid as possible. Use immediately, or let cool to room temperature, transfer to a glass jar, and refrigerate, tightly covered, for up to 2 months. Shake well before serving chilled, or gently reheat before serving.

peach, nectarine, apricot, or plum syrup

No matter what stone fruit I'm using, I like to add the pits to the mixture as it cooks for more flavor.

makes 2 cups

1 pound peaches, nectarines, apricots, or plums, chopped and pitted, pits reserved, or
12 ounces thawed frozen sliced peaches (about 2¼ cups)
½ cup sugar
½ cup light corn syrup
1 tablespoon fresh lemon juice
Pinch of salt

1. Bring the peaches, their pits, 1 cup water, the sugar, and the corn syrup to a boil in a large saucepan over medium-high heat, stirring until the sugar is dissolved. Continue to boil for 10 minutes. Remove from the heat and stir in the lemon juice and salt.

2. Pour the syrup through a large coarse strainer set over a bowl, pressing hard on the solids to extract as much liquid as possible. Use immediately, or let cool to room temperature, transfer to a glass jar, and refrigerate, tightly covered, for up to 2 months. Shake well before serving chilled, or gently reheat before serving.

CHERRY SYRUP

Cooking the pits with the cherries adds more flavor (you'll be straining the syrup anyway).

MAKES 2 CUPS

12 ounces (2 cups) ripe Bing cherries, halved and
    pitted, pits reserved
½ cup sugar
½ cup light corn syrup
1 tablespoon fresh lemon juice
Pinch of salt

1. Bring the cherries, their pits, 1 cup water, the sugar, and the corn syrup to a boil in a large saucepan over medium-high heat, stirring until the sugar is dissolved. Continue to boil for 10 minutes. Remove from the heat and stir in the lemon juice and salt.

2. Pour the syrup through a large coarse strainer set over a bowl, pressing hard on the solids to extract as much liquid as possible. Use immediately, or let cool to room temperature, transfer to a glass jar, and refrigerate, tightly covered, for up to 2 months. Shake well before serving chilled, or gently reheat before serving.

LEMON SYRUP

This makes a terrific soda with vanilla ice cream and seltzer. Or stir fresh berries or cut fruit into the lemon syrup. You can even use it to make lemonade—just add water and ice.

MAKES 1½ CUPS

½ teaspoon finely grated lemon zest
¾ cup fresh lemon juice (from about 3 large
    lemons)
½ cup sugar
½ cup light corn syrup
Pinch of salt

1. Bring the lemon zest, juice, ½ cup water, the sugar, and the corn syrup to a boil in a medium saucepan over high heat, stirring until the sugar is dissolved. Reduce the heat and simmer for 5 minutes.

2. Pour the syrup through a fine strainer set over a bowl. Let cool to room temperature, transfer to a glass jar, and refrigerate, tightly covered, for up to 2 months. Shake well before serving chilled.

VARIATION

If you'd like, replace some of the lemon juice with fresh lime juice and add a pinch of lime zest.

orange syrup

Perfect as a drizzle for Toasted Pound Cake (page 143) topped with scoops of orange sorbet and vanilla ice cream, this syrup has a wonderful fresh, clean orange flavor.

MAKES 1 CUP

Pinch of finely grated orange zest
1 cup fresh orange juice
⅓ cup light corn syrup
¼ cup sugar
Pinch of salt

1. Bring the orange zest, juice, corn syrup, and sugar to a boil in a medium saucepan over medium-high heat, stirring until the sugar is dissolved. Reduce the heat and simmer for 4 minutes. Remove from the heat and add the salt.

2. Pour the syrup through a fine strainer set over a bowl. Let cool to room temperature, transfer to a glass jar, and refrigerate, tightly covered, for up to 1 month. Shake well before serving chilled.

red grape syrup

Here's a much-simplified version of the fresh grape syrup known as sapa *in Italy. You might enjoy a syrup like this in the Emilia-Romagna region; in fact, it is thought that balsamic vinegar, from that same region, was born of* sapa *that was left to age for years in vinegar casks. I've had the syrup on panna cotta, which was splendid, but I think it's best over vanilla gelato. It's great for kids; they love its unusual color, almost Day-Glo grape.*

MAKES 2 CUPS

2 pounds red seedless grapes, stemmed
½ cup sugar
Pinch of salt

1. Bring the grapes, 2 cups water, and the sugar to a boil in a large saucepan over medium-high heat, stirring until the sugar is dissolved. Continue to boil for 10 minutes. Remove from the heat and stir in the salt.

2. Pour the syrup through a large fine strainer set over a bowl, pressing hard on the solids to extract as much liquid as possible. Use immediately, or let cool to room temperature, transfer to a glass jar, and refrigerate, tightly covered, for up to 1 month. Shake well before serving chilled, or gently reheat before serving.

passion fruit syrup

Use any frozen tropical fruit puree; my other favorites are guanabana, mora (like blackberry), and mango. Look for these purees in plastic bags in the freezer section of your supermarket.

MAKES 2 CUPS

½ cup sugar
½ cup light corn syrup
½ cup well-stirred thawed frozen passion fruit
    puree
Pinch of salt

1.   Bring 1 cup water, the sugar, and the corn syrup to a boil in a large saucepan over medium-high heat, stirring until the sugar is dissolved. Add the passion fruit puree, reduce the heat, and simmer for 3 minutes. Remove from the heat and stir in the salt.
2.   Let cool to room temperature, then transfer to a glass jar and refrigerate, tightly covered, for up to 2 months. Shake well before serving chilled.

mango syrup

Add the mango pit to the mixture as it cooks; it will give the syrup a bit more flavor. If really ripe fragrant mangoes aren't available, use frozen mango puree to make the syrup, following the previous recipe for Passion Fruit Syrup.

MAKES 2 CUPS

1 large ripe mango, peeled and chopped,
    pit reserved
½ cup sugar
½ cup light corn syrup
1 tablespoon fresh lime or lemon juice
Pinch of salt

1.   Bring the chopped mango, its pit, 1 cup water, the sugar, and the corn syrup to a boil in a large saucepan over medium-high heat, stirring until the sugar is dissolved. Reduce the heat and simmer for 10 minutes. Remove from the heat and stir in the lime juice and salt.
2.   Pour the syrup through a large coarse strainer set over a bowl, pressing hard on the solids to extract as much liquid as possible. Let cool to room temperature, transfer to a glass jar, and refrigerate, tightly covered, for up to 3 days. Shake well before serving chilled.

GINGER SYRUP

Use this to make an ice cream soda with coconut, mango, or pineapple ice cream.

MAKES 1½ CUPS

½ cup sugar
½ cup light corn syrup
½ cup finely chopped crystallized ginger
8 black peppercorns
A squeeze of fresh lime juice

1.   Bring 1 cup water, the sugar, corn syrup, ginger, and peppercorns to a boil in a medium saucepan over medium-high heat, stirring until the sugar is dissolved. Continue to boil for 5 minutes. Remove from the heat and stir in the lime juice.

2.   Pour the syrup through a large coarse strainer set over a bowl, pressing hard on the solids to extract as much liquid as possible. Let cool to room temperature, transfer to a glass jar, and refrigerate, tightly covered, for up to 1 month. Shake well before serving chilled.

TOASTED COCONUT SYRUP

This needs to be shaken very well before using because it tends to separate.

MAKES 1 CUP

¾ cup sweetened shredded coconut
¼ cup light corn syrup
A squeeze of fresh lime or lemon juice

1.   Preheat the oven to 375 degrees F. Spread the coconut on a baking sheet and toast, stirring once or twice, for 7 to 9 minutes, or until medium golden brown. Cool in the pan on a wire rack.

2.   Bring 1 cup water, the coconut, and the corn syrup to a boil in a medium saucepan over medium-high heat. Continue to boil for 10 minutes. Remove from the heat and stir in the lime juice.

3.   Pour the syrup through a coarse strainer set over a bowl, pressing hard on the solids to extract as much liquid as possible. Let cool to room temperature, transfer to a glass jar, and refrigerate, tightly covered, for up to 1 month. Shake vigorously before serving chilled.

LIQUEUR SYRUP

Elegant over a simple bowl of ice cream or gelato. Depending on the liqueur, you might prefer to use fruit juice or coffee instead of the water. The 3 tablespoons (1½ ounces) called for here is the size of most miniature bottles, also called nips or airline bottles, so you don't have to buy a large bottle. Try any of these popular liqueurs: Alizé (passion fruit and Cognac), amaretto, anisette, apple or sour apple, apricot, Bénédictine, blackberry, Chartreuse, cherry, chocolate, chocolate cherry, coffee, crème de cassis (black currant), crème de menthe, Drambuie, Galliano, ginger, Goldwasser (caraway and orange), hazelnut, Irish cream, Jägermeister, limoncello, maraschino, Midori, orange, Strega, or Vandermint (chocolate mint).

makes 1½ cups

½ cup sugar
½ cup light corn syrup
3 tablespoons liqueur
Pinch of salt

1. Bring 1 cup water, the sugar, and the corn syrup to a boil in a medium saucepan over medium-high heat, stirring until the sugar is dissolved. Continue to boil for 8 minutes. Remove from the heat and add the liqueur and salt.

2. Use immediately, or let cool to room temperature, transfer to a glass jar, and refrigerate, tightly covered, for up to several months. Shake well before serving chilled, or gently reheat before serving.

SLIGHTLY SWEETENED WHIPPED CREAM

It doesn't get more voluptuous than this. If the other ingredients in the dessert are all really sweet, use the lesser amount of sugar so the whipped cream will balance that sweetness— or vice versa. For the variations, start with the lesser amounts of flavorings, and add more in small increments until you get just the flavor you want. If you can find it, use cream that has not been ultrapasteurized. Ultrapasteurizing heats the cream to 280 degrees F for at least 2 seconds, extending its shelf life but compromising its fresh flavor and making it more difficult to whip.

MAKES ABOUT 2 CUPS

1 cup heavy cream
1 to 2 tablespoons confectioners' sugar
½ teaspoon pure vanilla extract

In a large deep bowl, beat the cream with an electric mixer on medium-high speed just until it begins to thicken. Add the sugar to taste and the vanilla (and/or the flavorings in the following variations) and beat just until the cream forms soft peaks when the beaters are lifted. The whipped cream can be made up to 4 hours ahead, tightly covered, and refrigerated. Whisk a few times if it starts to separate.

VARIATIONS

Sweetened whipped cream can be flavored with just about anything your heart desires. Feel free to combine any of the flavors in these variations. You might like strawberry and lemon, coffee and anise extract, passion fruit and orange, coconut and lime, or raspberry and crème de cassis.

Fruit or berry: Add fruit or berry sauces to taste or 6 to 8 tablespoons of any sweetened or unsweetened fruit or berry puree, such as strawberry, raspberry, peach or nectarine, cherry, plum, mango, pineapple, or apricot. Add sugar to taste, depending on the sweetness of the puree.

Lemon, orange, or lime: Add 1 tablespoon finely grated lemon zest, ½ to 1 teaspoon lime zest, or ½ to 1 teaspoon orange zest, and use 2 tablespoons confectioners' sugar. Or add the tiniest smidgen of a Boyajian pure citrus oil, or use Lemon Syrup (page 204) or Orange Syrup (page 205).

Passion fruit or other tropical fruit: Frozen tropical fruit purees are available in many supermarkets, especially Latino ones, and most of them are unsweetened. Try passion fruit mango, *mora* (like blackberry), guanabana, etc.—but stay away from the dark brown ones like tamarind that will tend to give the cream an unappealing look. Whip in 3 to 4 tablespoons well-stirred thawed frozen puree, and use 3 to 4 tablespoons sugar.

Concentrated fruit syrup: Available in supermarkets and health food stores, these are very intensely flavored syrups, quite sweet even though they usually contain no added sugar. Add 2 to 3 tablespoons of the syrup; you'll need little sugar, if any.

Chocolate: Add ¼ cup or so chilled Chocolate Syrup (page 198) or store-bought chocolate syrup, or to taste; you probably won't need any sugar or vanilla.

Cocoa: Sift in 3 to 4 tablespoons unsweetened cocoa powder, and increase the sugar to 4 to 6 tablespoons.

Chocolate malt: Use 5 to 6 tablespoons chocolate-flavored Ovaltine or other chocolate-flavored malted milk powder; omit the sugar and vanilla.

Coffee: Dissolve 2 teaspoons instant espresso powder in 1 teaspoon hot water and let cool. Use 3 to 4 tablespoons sugar, and add the espresso with the vanilla, or add Coffee Syrup (page 200).

Mocha: You have two choices, one using cocoa and one using chocolate. For the cocoa variation, dissolve 2 teaspoons instant espresso powder in 1 teaspoon hot water and let cool. Whip the cream using 4 to 6 tablespoons sugar and sift in 3 to 4 tablespoons unsweetened cocoa powder, adding the espresso with the vanilla. Or use the dissolved instant espresso powder with ¼ cup chilled Chocolate Syrup (page 198) or store-bought chocolate syrup, or to taste, and skip the sugar and vanilla.

Caramel or butterscotch: Omit the sugar, and fold 2 to 4 tablespoons room-temperature Old-fashioned Caramel Sauce (page 181), Scottish-Style Butterscotch Sauce (page 183), or store-bought caramel or butterscotch sauce into the whipped cream.

Coconut: Omit the vanilla, and use just a little sugar. Fold about 6 tablespoons toasted sweetened shredded coconut into the whipped cream, or fold in 2 to 4 tablespoons Toasted Coconut Syrup (page 207).

Ginger: Fold 1 to 2 tablespoons minced crystallized ginger into the whipped cream, or 2 to 4 tablespoons Ginger Syrup (page 207).

Spice: Add ground allspice, nutmeg, mace, cinnamon, cardamom, cloves, or another favorite spice to taste—start with an extra-large pinch.

Rose water or orange-flower water: Add 2 to 3 teaspoons; I like this best without the vanilla, which tends to overwhelm the delicate flower flavor and aroma.

Extract: Add ½ teaspoon or so of another pure extract instead of the vanilla (never use imitation flavors). You can add a bit more, but go easy—it's strong stuff. Anise extract is especially good with a coffee ice cream dessert—think Sambuca and coffee.

Spirit or liqueur: Add 2 to 3 tablespoons Cognac, rum, bourbon, eau-de-vie, liqueur, or fruit brandy; if what you're adding is sweet, go easy on the sugar, or don't use any at all.

- Soft peaks: When the beaters are lifted, the cream forms downy peaks that collapse within seconds.
- Stiff peaks: The beaters leave a path in the cream, and when they are lifted, the cream forms firm peaks that hold their shape.

about the author

LORI LONGBOTHAM, a graduate of the Culinary Institute of America, is the author of *Luscious Lemon Desserts* and *Lemon Zest: 175 Recipes with a Twist* and was the contributing editor to *The Dean and DeLuca Cookbook* and a contributor to the latest *Joy of Cooking*. Her work has been published in food and women's magazines, and other publications from *The New York Times Magazine* to *Prevention*. She has written for *Martha Stewart Living, Gourmet, Fitness, Good Housekeeping*, and many additional publications. Formerly food editor at *Gourmet* magazine, Longbotham has also worked as a caterer, private chef, and restaurant chef. She lives in Jackson Heights, New York. Her website address is www.lorilongbotham.com.